T0245726

Jewish Women in Time and Torah

JEWISH WOMEN IN TIME AND TORAH

ELIEZER BERKOVITS

Foreword by

RAḤEL BERKOVITS

URIM PUBLICATIONS

KTAV PUBLISHING

Dedicated to

Belda Lindenbaum

and our daughters, Victoria and Abigail.

May this work serve all who strive for
קדושה through learning

A Loving Husband and Friend

Jewish Women in Time and Torah
by Eliezer Berkovits
Foreword by Raḥel Berkovits
Second Edition

Originally published in 1990 by Ktav Publishing House
Copyright © 2022, 1990 Berkovits Family
All rights reserved. Printed in Israel.

No part of this book may be used or reproduced in any manner whatsoever without written permission from the copyright owner, except in the case of brief quotations embodied in reviews and articles.

Typeset by Juliet Tresgallo
ISBN 978-965-524-365-9

Urim Publications, P.O. Box 52287, Jerusalem 9152102 Israel
www.UrimPublications.com www.Ktav.com

The Library of Congress has cataloged the original edition as follows:
Names: Berkovits, Eliezer, 1908-1992, author.
Title: Jewish women in time and Torah / Eliezer Berkovits.
Description: First edition. | Hoboken, N.J.: KTAV Pub. House, [1990]
| Includes bibliographical references and index.
Identifiers: LCCN 89049044 | ISBN 0881253111 (hardcover)
Subjects: Women in Judaism. | Women – Legal status, laws, etc. (Jewish law).
Classification: BM729.W6 B37 1990 | DDC 296/.082
LC record available at https://lccn.loc.gov/89049044

In loving memory of our mother, **Sali Berkovits** *a"h*
beloved wife of Avraham, **Elya Ruben Berkovits** *a"h*
and dear mother-in-law of Shimshon, **Ruth Fortgang** *a"h*

Dov Berkovits

Shimshon Berkovits

Avraham Berkovits

Contents

Foreword by Raḥel Berkovits 9
Author's Foreword 17

I. "Women Are a People by Themselves"

1. The Nonpersonal Status 19
2. Marriage and Divorce 23
3. Social Exclusion 29
4. Opinions 34
5. Time and Torah 35
6. Torah-Tolerated, Not Torah-Taught 49

II. Woman as a Person

1. Torah Ideals and Teaching 55
2. Halakhic Innovations 58

III. "In the Midst of My People I Dwell" 71

IV. Contemporary Halakhic Issues Regarding Women

1. Self-Obligation by Women 81
2. Women's Prayer Services 85
3. *Birkhat ha-Mazon* 93
4. Saying *Kiddush* and Reading the Megillah 102
5. Talmudic and Halakhic Efforts to Improve the Wife's Status in Relationship to Her Husband 109
6. The Agunah Problem 120

V. Conclusions 135

Glossary 141

FOREWORD

Raḥel Berkovits

When *Jewish Women in Time and Torah* was first published over thirty years ago, I was at the beginning of my journey as a young woman struggling to find my place within the world of Torah and halakhah. At that point, women had been learning Talmud and other basic Jewish texts at a high level for a good number of years and were now yearning to turn that knowledge into personal practice of *mitzvot*, some of which were denied to women. We wanted to be active participants in the ritual that formed the fabric of our personal lives and that of our communities. At times we felt alienated and neglected by traditional Judaism and its leaders.

I was in college, seriously thinking about these issues, when *Jewish Women in Time and Torah* was released. I was pleased, fascinated, and touched that my very own grandfather had written on an issue so close to my heart – the status of women in halakhic Judaism. What perplexed me at the time was his motivation. What motivated him to dedicate a whole book to this topic? Clearly he himself was not a woman trying to reconcile what she knew about herself and what the texts of tradition said about her gender. My grandfather, father to three sons, did not even have any daughters, and thus could not witness their struggles firsthand. And although my grandmother was an incredibly strong and individualistic character, her activism did not lie within the halakhic context.[1]

1. I very clearly remember eating Shabbat lunch at my grandmother's with my brother after my grandfather had passed away. At the end of the meal when I suggested that we have a mixed *zimmun* (as my grandfather discusses in this book on pages 98–102), my grandmother said very forcefully, "Not in my house we don't!"

Nor was my grandfather a young rabbi at the start of his career, hoping to make a name for himself, and so chose to write on the pressing hot topic of the day. I was baffled – what motivates an eighty-year-old traditional European rabbi to write an innovative and progressive treatise on the status of women in halakhic Judaism at a time when most other Orthodox rabbis are not even willing to admit there is a problem? However, as I came to understand my grandfather's commitment to *Torat Hayyim* – a living eternal Torah – I realized that this work on women's status was a fitting culmination to his vast teaching and writing career.

This book is an outgrowth of Rabbi Professor Eliezer Berkovits' theology and belief system. His philosophical understanding of the nature and function of the halakhic system shaped his view on the status of women in Judaism, and his role as a *posek* compelled him to address their religious needs in the modern day. This progression and development can be seen in his published works. Besides the entire volume he wrote on marriage and divorce law,[2] the topic of women appeared throughout his books and articles,[3] and so it was only natural that he decided to dedicate this entire book to the topic. In *Crisis and Faith*,[4] published in 1976, Berkovits entitled the seventh chapter "The Status of Women within Judaism," and seven years later he devoted the first chapter of his magnum opus *Not in Heaven: The Nature and Function of Halakha* to "The Halakhic Conscience and the Status of the Woman."[5] Finally, here in *Jewish Women in Time and Torah*,[6] the last of his nineteen books, Berkovits addressed the issue head-on. He presented

2. תנאי בנשואין ובגט (*Conditionality in Marriage and Divorce*), Jerusalem: *Mosad Harav Kook*, 1966 and 2008.

3. "מעמד האשה ביהדות – הבט הלכתי-חברתי" ("The Status of Women in Judaism: A Socio-Halakhic Overview") *Hagot* 5, *Misrad Hahinuch*, 1983, pp. 27–34.

"התחייבות עצמית של נשים במצות עשה שהזמן גרמא" ("The Self-Obligation of Women in Positive Time Caused Commandments"), *Sinai* 100, 1987, pp. 187–94.

4. *Crisis and Faith*, Chapter 7, "The Status of Women within Judaism," New York: Sanhedrin, 1976.

5. *Not in Heaven: The Nature and Function of Halakha*, Chapter 1, "The Halakhic Conscience and the Status of the Woman," Chapter 4, "Marriage and Divorce Laws." New York: Ktav, 1983.

6. First published by Ktav Publishing, Hoboken, NJ: 1990.

his theological explanation for a woman's status in past generations, and the changes that are possible in the present day.

Berkovits' views on women are the product of his philosophy of halakhah in general and his understanding of the nature of *Torat Hayyim* in particular. A number of the examples of halakhic ingenuity which appear in the Mishnah and Talmud involve women and divorce. These cases helped Berkovits form his general views of the nature and function of halakhah and in turn caused him to grapple seriously and practically with the issue in modern times – for Berkovits believed that a living Torah must speak to the unique needs of each specific generation. As he explains: "The Torah is eternal because it has a Word for each generation… One can find the Word that has been waiting for this hour to be revealed only if one faces the challenges of each new situation in the history of the generations of Israel and attempts to deal with it in intellectual and ethical honesty."[7]

Berkovits' deep commitment to and faith in the eternity and truth of the Divine Torah left him no other choice in his role as a *posek* but to take responsibility to act and thus fulfill what he thought was his part in the covenant with God. For Berkovits, the study of halakhah was not confined to the walls of the *beit midrash.* He writes: "There is no halakhah of the ivory tower. The attitude to human needs is decisive. Without understanding, without sympathy and compassion, one cannot be an authentic halakhist."[8]

This great sensitivity to, and deep understanding of, human reality and need, compelled Berkovits to speak out regarding women's issues. He courageously voiced what he believed to be halakhic truth without concern for normative communal labels or how his views would be received by the establishment. For example, in a letter to the editor of the Jerusalem Post newspaper, he staunchly defended women's prayer groups after the leadership of Yeshiva University had condemned them, and he voiced public support for the women who participated in them:

7. *Not in Heaven*, pp. 117–8.
8. *Crisis and Faith*, p. 98.

> Sir – I read with interest your article of September 11, "Orthodox women fume at rabbis." One may no longer remain silent. I have read carefully the responsum of the five Talmudists at Yeshiva University, forbidding prayer services by women. I wish to state unequivocally that their so called "T'shuva" has nothing to do with Halacha.
>
> People will have to realize that knowledge and understanding are not identical. One may know a lot and understand very little.
>
> There may be a great deal of Orthodoxy around. Unfortunately, there is only very little halakhic Judaism.
>
> May God grant to the women of the Women's Tefilla Network strength and courage to continue their efforts to the best of their abilities.[9]

Berkovits' views on women and his motivation to speak out and create change also stemmed from his most basic core belief about the Divine. In one of his Hebrew articles he uses a Tanaitic midrash about the daughters of Zelophehad to explain his own behavior:

> I think that the time has come to admit the truth and to confess that in the legal-halakhic area as well as in the communal-sociological area there is severe inequality to the detriment of women.
>
> Interestingly, *Hazal* themselves were aware of this situation. In order to substantiate my remarks, I will quote from the *Sifrei* on the verse: "The daughters of Zelophehad came forward… They stood before Moses" (*Numbers* 27:1–2).[10] The *Sifrei* says: "Since the daughters of Zelophehad heard that the land would be divided [amongst] the tribes, [and given] to the males and not to the females, they all gathered to take advice one from the other. They said: The compassion of God is not like the compassion of human beings [literally, flesh and blood]. Human beings have more compassion on males than on females. But the One who spoke and the world came into existence is not so. Rather God has compassion on males and on females. God has compassion on everything." We hear a kind of

9. Letter to the editor, *Jerusalem Post*, April 1, 1985.
10. *Sifrei Bamidbar* #133.

> criticism, which *Hazal* themselves have leveled, about the laws of the division of the land. Seemingly the issue is very simple. Because I believe in the Holy One Blessed be He and because I believe that the Holy One Blessed be He has compassion on all his creations – for this reason all discrimination is forbidden to me. I am obligated to cleave to his deeds.[11]

Berkovits' fundamental belief that God, as the creator of the world and humanity, does not discriminate between the genders, and his belief that his role as a Jew and *posek* was to emulate the Divine must be a central aspect of what drove him to write this book. In it he provides a profound theological explanation for why one should always be working towards elevating women to their "Torah true" place of equality despite very clear and disparaging statements, which relegate them to a second-class legal status within the Torah and rabbinic literature. His treatise reconciles those discriminatory Torah texts with the compassionate Giver of Torah who, as seen from the story of the daughters of Zelophehad, could never have ideally wanted to favor men over women.

Belief not only in God but in the Divine's Torah and eternal system of halakhah, was another aspect of Berkovits' worldview that led him to address women's issues. In a private correspondence to his Rebbe, R. Yechiel Yaakov Weinberg, the *Sridei Esh*, regarding the problem of *agunot*, women chained in marriage, he writes: "I believe with complete faith that there is a solution because I believe. Because I believe in the

11. *Maamad HaIsha Beyahadut – Mabat Hilkhati- Hevrati*, p. 27–8. The translation is my own. The original reads:
אני חושב שהגיע הזמן להודות על האמת ולהתוודות, שבשטח המשפטי-הילכתי וגם בשטח החברתי-סוציולוגי שורר אי-שוויון חמור לרעת האשה. מעניין הוא, שחז״ל בעצמם היו מודעים למצב זה. בכדי לבסס את דברי, אצטט מה׳ספרי׳ על הפסוק: ״ותקרבנה בנות צלפחד... ותעמדנה לפני משה״ (במדבר כ״ז א׳). אומר ה׳ספרי׳: ״ותקרבנה בנות צלפחד״ (במדבר פרק כז:א) כיון ששמעו בנות צלפחד שהארץ מתחלקת לשבטים, לזכרים ולא לנקבות, נתקבצו כולן זו על זו ליטול עצה. אמרו: ״לא כרחמי בשר ודם, רחמי המקום. בשר ודם רחמיו על הזכרים יותר מן הנקבות אבל מי שאמר והיה העולם, אינו כן אלא רחמיו על הזכרים ועל הנקבות רחמיו על הכל.״ שומעים אנו מעין ביקורת, שחז״ל בעצמם מתחו, על דיני חלוקת הארץ. לכאורה הדבר פשוט מאוד. מכיוון שאני מאמין בקב״ה ומכיוון שאני מאמין שהקדוש ברוך הוא רחמיו על כל מעשיו – מטעם זה כל הפליה אסורה עלי. אני מחויב לבדוק במעשיו.

God of Israel and his Torah, I also believe in the strength and eternal power of the Halakhah to solve the problems that transpire in the lives of the *Am Yisrael*."[12]

This belief that halakhah must find a solution for the intolerable situation of women who are *agunot* spurred Berkovits to write a halakhic treatise on the issue in 1966, well before other leading rabbinic figure were willing to address the issue. He describes his experiences and motivation for that book in the same Hebrew article cited above.

> Interestingly, before the publication of the book, one of the senior rabbis in the United States[13] gave the manuscript to one of the great rabbinic authorities [*poskim*] in the United States and the entire world so that he could offer his opinion.[14] And this was his response: "From the side of halakha I have no reason to oppose, but if one should do [*la'asot*] this – that is already a different issue."
>
> What we need to understand today is that it is "a time to act" [*et la'asot*] and it is "a time to act" not just for the woman but rather "a time to act for *HaShem*,"[15] for the things that are happening today are in the category of a desecration of God's name [*hillul HaShem*]. The role of halakha is to solve problems.[16]

12. The letter is undated and was most probably written around the early 1960s. The translation is mine. The original reads:
אני מאמין באמונה שלמה שיש פתרון מפני שאני מאמין. מפני שאני מאמין בא-להי ישראל ובתורתו אני מאמין ג״כ בכחו האיתן והנצחי של ההלכה לפתור את הבעיות העוברות את חיי עם ישראל.

13. I believe this is a reference to R. Leo Jung.

14. I believe this is a reference to R. Moshe Feinstein.

15. Psalms 119:126.

16. *Maamad HaIsha Beyahadut – Mabat Hilkhati- Hevrati*, p. 34. The translation is my own. The original reads:
מעניין, שלפני הדפסת הספר, מסר אחד מזקני הרבנים בארצות הברית את כתב-היד לאחד מגדולי הפוסקים בארצות הברית ובעולם כולו כדי שיחווה את דעתו. זו הייתה תשובתו: ״מצד ההלכה אין לי מה להתנגד, אבל אם לעשות את זה – זה כבר עניין אחר.״
מה שאנחנו צריכים להבין היום הוא ש״עת לעשות״, ו״עת לעשות״ לא רק בשביל האשה אלא ״עת לעשות לה׳״, מפני שהדברים שמתרחשים היום הם בבחינת חילול-השם. תפקידה של ההלכה הוא לעשות לפתרונן של בעיות.

Berkovits felt that to remain silent in the face of true human tragedy and not to actively search for a halakhic way to address the needs of women was a desecration of God's Holy Name. Directly opposing those who believe that to preserve the true and Godly nature of Torah there can be no change, Berkovits' whole life was dedicated to acting in the name of, and becoming a model of, *Hakadosh Barukh Hu*, in this human world so as to bring about a transformation in the attitudes toward and status of women in halakhic Judaism.

One could look back on these past thirty years since the original publication of this book and say that the innovations and advances that have ensued for women within the halakhic world are a celebration and tribute to the real life change Berkovits helped bring about with the writing of this important work. On the other hand, there is also a measure of sadness that this book remains so relevant today. There is so much work to be done to bring attention to the pain of *agunot*, to ensure that women can actively participate in both personal and communal ritual when they wish to, and to move beyond the negative and disparaging views that are still "Torah tolerated" in our communities to values that mirror the Divine and are authentically "Torah taught."

What is most important about this book, what makes it as relevant and new as the day it was first published, is not the specific halakhic cases and rituals that Berkovits so eruditely writes about, but rather the theology and philosophy of halakhah that he presents. This book offers a coherent argument for both how to uphold the eternal Divine nature of Torah and yet to also recognize that the ever-changing status of women, reflected in our sacred texts, is linked to historical and social movements of humanity in the greater world at large. The explanation Berkovits posits enables him to make halakhic suggestions for innovations within ritual despite past precedent of women's non-participation. The presentation of this world-view, which reflects looking at the issues with ethical and moral honesty, lends support and basis for present and future halakhists and *poskim* to initiate change in women's status and practice. Hopefully, this will not be seen as deviating from tradition but rather will be understood as a direct outgrowth of the true nature of Torah.

For my grandfather being an active part of women's historical and social change within the Jewish community was a reflection of who he was – a simple God-fearing Jew, committed with his whole being to the way of life of Torah, halakhah, and *mitzvot*. This book is a fitting crown and testament to his legacy.

May God grant us strength and courage to continue his efforts to the best of our abilities in pursuit of the "gradual halakhic renewal that will ultimately reestablish Judaism as *Torat Hayyim* – a Torah of Life."[17]

Jerusalem, Israel
Purim 5781/2021

17. See end of page 140.

Author's Foreword

It is not our intention in this work to plead the cause of Jewish women against the numerous Jewish laws that today are rightly considered unfair or even unjust; nor do we intend to defend Judaism against criticism for its treatment of women. The aim is neither to be critical nor to be apologetic; but on the basis of our understanding to unravel the truth, from the aggadic and halakhic sources, of some of the fundamental principles of Judaism.

If we seek truth and understanding, we must realize that because we are living in a different era, we may not be in a position to evaluate the significance of the mores and laws that appear in the traditional Jewish sources. The changes since biblical and Talmudic times have been radical. Women and men today are not the same as the women and men who lived, worked, planned, and hoped many centuries ago. Conditions of life, reality, social order, aspirations, and goals have changed fundamentally. If we criticize, we may not know what we criticize; if we defend, we may have no idea what we defend.

However, awareness of the changes over time is not enough. One must also have an adequate understanding of the system of Judaism as it treats the time-conditioned reality of the life of the people.

There were essentially three distinct phases in the evolving status of Jewish women. The first phase was Torah-tolerated rather than Torah-established or Torah-taught. It derived from the mores, conditions, and circumstances of an early age, and was not essentially different from what we find in other societies in the same stage of development. Women's status in this era was nonpersonal. While it could not be changed overnight by legislation, certain limited changes were effected to indicate the direction of the kind of development the Torah desired. The second phase established woman's personal status. And finally, in our discussion of the third phase, we attempt to clarify some of the consequences of the Torah-teaching and halakhic principles for the present status of women.

Most of the material in the last section of the fourth chapter is dealt with in chapter 2 under "Halakhic Innovations." However, because of the importance of the subject for the contemporary situation, we present it apart from the interpretive context of the discussion.

I "Women Are a People by Themselves"

(T. Bavli, *Shabbat* 62a)

1. THE NONPERSONAL STATUS

Before entering into a discussion of specific laws and mores, it will be advisable to examine the status that women had in the early centuries of Jewish antiquity and the centuries immediately following. How are they seen and evaluated? One of the earliest statements about women is found in the words of the prophet Jeremiah: "The mighty men of Babylon stopped waging war. They sit in fortresses. Their strength has left them. They have become like women."[1] In other words, women are not just the weaker sex: they are weak. The consequences of this opinion are evident in the midrashic interpretation of several biblical verses. One of the most revealing is based on two words in the Book of Genesis, where we are told about Lamech: "And he begat a son."[2] The Midrash relates the Hebrew *ben*, "son," to the verb *banah*, which means "to build." And the explanation given is: "A son from whom the world was built." The son, of course, was Noah, who rebuilt the world after the flood, the idea being that sons, i.e., men, are the world-builders.[3] It may very well be that in antiquity and even centuries later, conditions were such that women, because of their nature, were not capable of "world-building." However, the situation thus established had most serious results for the treatment that women received in society. World-builders are, of course, also family-builders, and that is why a family is called

1. Jeremiah 51:30.
2. Genesis 5:28.
3. See Rashi, quoting Midrash Tanhuma, chap. 11.

after the father and not after the mother. The Talmudic formulation is: "The father's family is called a family; the mother's family is not called a family." The Talmud bases this determination on a verse at the beginning of the Book of Numbers, where Moses is asked by God to count the heads of the community of the children of Israel "according to their families, their fathers' houses."[4] Obviously, this is the origin of the widespread expression "my father's house" (note that there is no comparable "my mother's house"). The interpretation justifies certain aspects of the inheritance law which are rather discriminatory against the women in the family.

Another most revealing statement about the treatment that women received in early Jewish society is found in a mishnah: "The man has precedence over the woman to be maintained."[5] This means that if both are in danger of their lives, e.g., if both are in equal danger of drowning, the man is to be saved first. Maimonides explains that since the man is obligated to observe more *mitzvot* (divine commandments) than the woman, his life is of greater sanctity than the woman's.[6] It is not our intention to enter into a discussion of the reasons for the exemption of women from the obligation to observe *mitzvot aseh she-hazeman geramah*, commandments whose observance is dependent on certain times of the day or the season. Aside from that, this law means that the life of a woman is less valuable than that of a man and, therefore, is more easily dispensed with. Not only does woman, at this stage, not have equal status with man in this male-built society, but she is really outside of it.

Suffice it to cite just two halakhic discussions that have a bearing on this subject. Women are obligated to say *Birkat ha-Mazon* (grace after meals). The Talmud asks, however, whether this obligation is of biblical origin or is based on a rabbinic innovation. The question requires an explanation: Why should it be a rabbinical commandment? The Bible says clearly: "And you shall eat and be satisfied, and you shall bless the

4. Bava Batra 109b.
5. Horayot 13a.
6. Maimonides, Commentary on the Mishnah, ibid.

Eternal One, your God."[7] Surely this is not an obligation dependent on the time of day. Why should women not be obligated to recite grace as a biblical mitzvah? The reason this question arises is explained in the commentaries of Rashi and Tosafot. According to Rashi, the command to say grace does not seem to apply to women because after the words "and you shall bless the Eternal One, your God" the Bible continues: "for the good land that He gave you," and as we know, the land was distributed among the male members of the tribes and women did not receive a share in it. How can they thank God for the "good land" if it was given to the men and not to them?

Tosafot does not agree with this explanation. Maintaining that the question is raised because in the *Birkat ha-Mazon* we thank God "for the covenant that You have sealed in our flesh [i.e., circumcision] and Your Torah that You have taught us," it notes that women are neither circumcised nor obligated to study Torah. In other words, they were not given the covenant and have not received the Torah.[8]

One cannot help wondering how such ideas could have entered the minds of the Talmudic authorities who made these statements! Is it really conceivable that since the sign of the covenant was the circumcision, the covenant was not concluded with all Israel, but only with its male members? Or is one supposed to imagine that since women were not obligated to study Torah, therefore the Torah was given only to the men and not to the Jewish people in its entirety? Would not the study of the Torah and the keeping of its commandments and listening to its teaching shape, indeed create, the Jewish people in its entirety? And as for Rashi's explanation, is it conceivable that the land, having been distributed among the male members, was not given as a divine blessing to the entire Jewish people? Do the numerous biblical promises that God will bring the children of Israel to a "land flowing with milk and honey" apply only to the male children but not to the female? Thank God, the woman's obligation to say grace, because of the biblical command, was accepted as halahkah, as the valid law. And yet the very idea why women ought to be excluded from the biblical command seems to be absurd.

7. Deuteronomy 8:10.
8. Rashi and Tosafot on Berakhot 20b.

Another aspect of the halakhic discussion of this subject may enlighten us. What real difference does it make whether women have a biblical or only a rabbinic obligation to say grace after a meal? Whatever the case may be, they are required to do it. The explanation given is based on the generally valid halakhic principle that one person may act for someone else to fulfill (certain) commandments if they are both under the same obligation. Thus, if a husband is unable to say grace, his wife can fulfill the commandment for him (assuming he was present and listening). But since the husband is obligated by the biblical command, his wife can only act for him if her obligation is also of biblical quality. However, if her obligation is only by rabbinic institution, she cannot function for her husband, since biblically she is not under any obligation. But now the question arises: in the case of *Birkat ha-Mazon*, an exception to the generally valid principle exists. The biblical obligation to say grace is dependent on one's having eaten a certain minimum amount of food. Strangely enough, according to the *din*, if a person has eaten less than the prescribed amount, his obligation is now reduced to the rabbinical level. Nevertheless, he may still recite the blessing for another man who has partaken of the required amount of food that determines his obligation by biblical command.

A further question is now justified: even if a woman's grace obligation is only rabbinical, why should a wife not be able to recite the blessings after the meal, even if her husband's obligation is of biblical force? And now comes the quite surprising and hardly believable explanation. A man, in relation to another man, has to act in accordance with the principle that *kol Yisrael arevin zeh ba-zeh* ("all Israel are responsible for one another").[9] Since man has the additional obligation to assist another man to fulfill his biblical duty, he can function for another man even if, as in the case like this, his own obligation to say grace is only rabbinical.

Not so a woman, however. The principle that "all Israel are responsible for each other" does not apply to women.[10] Astounding! Are women really not included in *kol Yisrael* ("all Israel")? Is it even

9. Shavuot 39a.

10. See Rosh on Berakhot 20b.

imaginable that Jewish women are not under the obligation of mutual Jewish responsibility? How is it to be understood? The examples we have discussed seem to indicate that women were indeed not included as active participants in the society of "world-builders." The highest respect that is expressed for the role of women in society at that time is found in the words that Rav addressed to Rabbi Hiyya: "In what lies the merit of women? In bringing their children to the synagogue [where they used to study] and in letting their husbands go to the *bet hamidrash* [the house of higher Torah study] and in waiting up for them to return home from the *bet hamidrash*."[11] Certainly, this function of women deserves to be appreciated. In essence it means that the task of women was to assist, to help the "world-builders." In other words, their task was to serve.

2. MARRIAGE AND DIVORCE

Nothing gives clearer expression to the servile responsibility of women than the original laws of marriage and divorce. The principle upon which marriage was based is clearly formulated by Maimonides, who writes: "When a man espouses a wife, what he says to her should be clearly understood to mean that he is purchasing the woman and not that she conveys herself to him as his possession."[12] The expression he uses is related to a phrase in the first mishnah in Tractate *Kiddushin*, which begins with the words *ha-ishah nikneit*, "the woman is bought." According to the Talmudic interpretation, the law derives from the biblical phrase "when a man takes a wife."[13] In this context "to take" means to acquire possession. Otherwise, the word *mikadesh*, literally meaning "to sanctify," is used. By the act of *kiddushin* a man "separates" a woman from all other men unto himself. To this day, the marriage formula under the *huppah* is: *harei at mekudeshet li*, "you are sanctified / separated for me." The meaning is the same: "You belong to me, because

11. Berakhot 17a.
12. *Hilkhot Ishut* 3:1.
13. Deuteronomy 22:13.

I am acquiring you." However, "possession" here does not connote property as such, which applies only to slaves,[14] but means that the husband is buying the woman's services. Her main obligation is to bear his children. The commandment "Be fruitful and multiply" was given only to men, not to women. Thus, a man has to provide himself with a wife in order to fulfill the commandment. Since it is the husband who enacts the marriage, by acquiring the woman's services and thus making her his wife, only the husband can terminate the marriage. According to the law, no divorce may take place against the will of the husband. On the other hand, he may divorce his wife whenever it pleases him to do so. According to Rabbi Akiva, divorce is justified even on such frivolous grounds as the husband's finding another woman more pleasing to him than his wife.[15]

The legal form of marriage that hands the wife over into the power of her husband was in itself inadequate to serve as the foundation of marriage. The husband had to have some responsibilities toward his wife. Three basic ones are stated in the Bible: *she'erah, kesutah, ve-onatah*, i.e., the husband is required to provide his wife with food, clothing, household goods, and a place to live. Finally, he is also commanded not to withhold from her the satisfaction of the natural sexual needs of a normal woman. Beyond this, it is difficult to find in the Torah any other obligation of the husband towards his wife. We have the institution of the *ketubah* (marriage contract). But whether the *ketubah* is biblically prescribed or is one of the later *takkanot hakhamim* (rabbinical rulings) remains an unresolved issue in the Talmudic and the major commentaries.[16] Maimonides states unambiguously: "It was the scholars [*hakhamim*] who established the *ketubah* for the wife, so that it would not be easy for the husband to send her away."[17] The *ketubah* states the husband's contractual obligation to pay a certain sum of money to his wife if he divorces her. The sum itself was rabbinically

14. See, e.g., Kiddushin 7b.

15. Gittin 90a.

16. See Ketubot 110b, 39b, and 11a, mainly Tosafot; Sotah 27a, s. v. *ish, ish*; also Tosafot to Ketubot 10a, s. v. *amar R. Nahman.*

17. Ishut 10:7.

prescribed (i.e., 200 zuz or its equivalent), but the bride's relatives were free, before the marriage, to negotiate a more adequate compensation for the wife in case of divorce. The contract became legally binding for both sides.

On the other hand, the wife's responsibilities toward her husband were all based on *takkanot hakhamim* (rabbinical rulings). Since the husband had to provide his wife with her full sustenance, she was required to render certain domestic services to him. According to the Mishnah: "These are the services that a wife has to perform for her husband: grind, bake, wash, cook, nurse her child, prepare the bed for him, and work in wool." (She may be released from these duties in proportion to the number of maid-slaves that she brings with her into marriage.)[18]

It is important to note why such heavy duties were imposed upon the wife. According to the Talmudic sources, this was done in order to compensate the husband, in a sense, for the expense of providing daily sustenance for her. Even though this was required under biblical law, the Talmudic teachers realized that it was a rather one-sided obligation. It could give the marriage an ethically questionable character; emphasizing the *bought* character of the wife for the purpose of enabling the husband to fulfill the mitzvah of begetting children. On the other hand, a mutuality of obligation would introduce a personal element into the marriage. The wife would serve her husband in order to make herself beloved by him: *kedei shetekhabev et atzmah al ba'alah.*

The idea that the wife made herself beloved by her husband through the services she rendered him had far-reaching consequences. According to the mishnah quoted above, one of the wife's required duties was "to prepare the bed for him." Another Talmudic passage elaborates that according to rabbinical rule, the wife is free from the burden of this labor in direct proportion to the number of maid-servants (i.e., slaves) she brings with her into the marriage. If she brings four servants with her, she may sit in a *katedra* (a chair of dignified comfort)[19]. There is one kind of service from which she is not released, however. Maimonides

18. Ketubot 59b.
19. Ketubot 61a.

quotes Rabbi Isaac as follows: "Thus, every wife washes the face, hands, and feet of her husband; prepares for him the cup of wine (it was customary to mix wine with a measure of water); prepares the bed for him; stands before him and waits on him, for instance by handing him water, handing him utensils, or taking them from before him – and similar things."[20] Rashi explains: "The scholars gave her this advice to establish in Israel that she would be beloved by her husband. However, only in the case of a wife who, because of the number of her maid-servants is free from all other work, do the sages advise [her] to continue with these services."[21] In other cases, she has to render these services to her husband as part of her duties, not merely as a wise, rabbinically recommended policy. Another passage in Maimonides may be looked upon as the ultimate formulation of a wife's duties toward her husband, and at the same time as a clear indication of the status of women: "Thus they [the scholars] commanded that the wife should honor her husband beyond any limit, and his fear should be over her, and everything she does should be according to his demands. He should be in her eyes like a prince or a king who behaves in accordance with his heart's desires. She should remove everything that is hateful to him, etc."[22] According to the commentaries, this is based on the Talmudic passage in which a son raises the question: "If my father and my mother each ask me to bring them a glass of water, to whom should I bring the water first?" The answer is: "Serve your father first, for you and your mother are both required to honor him."[23] Maimonides' formulation is an elaboration of what is meant by the *kavod* (honor) due to the husband. It is an elaboration that was included in the wife's duties toward her husband. A summary of all these services and duties can be found in a midrashic statement: "Only a wife who fulfills the will of her husband is proper, worthy."[24] One wonders whether the purpose of such far-reaching service and honor is only to make the wife more beloved by her husband; is it

20. Ishut 21:3.
21. Ketubot 61b.
22. Ishut 15:20.
23. Kiddushin 31a.
24. Yalkut Shimoni, Shoftim 4, end of par. 42; see also Even ha-Ezer 369, Rema.

not also the necessary consequence of her inferior, serving status?

At this phase in the development of the laws of marriage, making oneself beloved falls essentially, and one-sidedly, upon the wife. Of course, corresponding to the responsibilities of the wife, the husband has to reciprocate. But how far that is from personalizing the marriage is easily seen in the light of the qualifications that some of these duties received. For instance, it was the husband's duty to provide medical care for his wife if she fell ill, but his responsibility had its limits. "If he sees that the sickness is a long-lasting one and he would lose much money, he may say to her: 'Here is your *ketubah*. Heal yourself with its value or else I divorce you.' And he may go." Adds Maimonides: "According to the law, the husband can do so, but it is not proper behavior [*derekh eretz*] to act in this manner."[25]

There were several similar rulings. A husband is required to redeem his wife if she is taken prisoner or kidnapped, but if the ransom demanded for her release is more than "her value" compared to the other prisoners, he need not redeem her. On the other hand, if the generally accepted ransom is far above the worth of her *ketubah*, he cannot say: "I am divorcing her. Here is her *ketubah*, let her go and redeem herself." In such a case he is compelled to redeem her, even if the sum demanded is as much as ten times the value of her *ketubah*. And even if the ransom demanded represents everything he possesses. However, if the husband redeems his wife as prescribed and she falls into captivity a second time, he may then, if he wishes, divorce her and pay her the value of her *ketubah*, and it is up to her to redeem herself.[26]

Laws of this kind show that the services the wife has to render in order to make herself beloved by her husband, thus introducing a personal element into the utterly impersonal marriage arrangements, are quite one-sided. The laws we have cited prove that the personal element, intimacy, is still lacking in this kind of marriage.

It could not have been otherwise, because of the wife's complete dependence on her husband. Her obligation to do all the work we have indicated was extended into the general principle that her earnings

25. Ishut 14:17.
26. Ibid., par. 19.

belonged to her husband. Beyond that, even what she might happen to find became his possession.[27] The rationale for this ruling is similar to the one that justified the wife's performing services for her husband – in order to protect her against possible hatred by him. This, however, leads us to a much wider principle: "Whatever a wife acquires is acquired by her husband."[28] In keeping with these rules, the law of inheritance follows logically. Accordingly, if the wife dies, the husband inherits her property (i.e., property that she brought into the marriage or received after the marriage as a gift or inheritance); but if he dies, she does not inherit him. (We need not enter into the discussion of whether this is a biblical rule or a later rabbinical arrangement.)[29]

According to the Talmud, the Torah was aware of the wife's almost total dependence on her husband. The thought is based on the verse Leviticus 19:2, "One should fear one's mother and father." In the Hebrew verse, "one" is expressed by the word *ish*, which means "a man." Is a woman, then, not obliged "to fear" her parents? The question is answered by the grammatical form of the word "should fear," which in the Hebrew original is *tira'u*, the plural. Why? Obviously, because the Torah wishes to say: "Both of you, man and woman, should fear your parents." Why then, asks the Talmud, does the verse begin with the singular *ish*? It answers: The emphasis is on the man because he has the power to do it, and not on the woman, because she is under the authority of others. Explains Rashi: "He has the power because no one may object to his intention; but a husband may prevent his wife from doing what is demanded of her."[30]

One may, of course, ask the question: If a wife is required to serve her husband, is she not much different from a slave? The very phrase "what a woman acquires belongs to her husband" is exactly the same as that asserted about a slave: "What a slave acquires belongs to his master." (It also appears in the formulation: "A slave cannot acquire anything without his master, a woman cannot acquire anything without

27. Ketubot 65b.
28. Nazir 24, Gittin 77a, etc.
29. Bava Batra 111b.
30. Rashi to Kiddushin 20b.

her husband," i.e., in both cases, the acquisition is the master's.)

Indeed, Rashi explains a discussion in the Talmud on the basis of the identity of these phrases: "For a wife is like a slave, for her husband possesses the work of her hands and whatever she may find, just as the master of a slave has the same right to the acquisition by a slave."[31] It is worth noting that the Talmud was fully aware of the similarity between the position of the slave and the wife.

In the introductory part of the morning service a male person says blessings. In one he thanks God for not making him a slave; in the other for not making him a woman. The question arises: what need is there for the first blessing, on not having been created a slave, since the same gratitude is expressed in the second blessing when one thanks God for not having made one a woman? Explains Rashi: "For the wife serves her husband like a maid-servant, like a slave his master." The answer does not change much in the wife's status, though he also says: "Nevertheless, the status of a slave is still somewhat lower."[32]

3. SOCIAL EXCLUSION

No wonder that such evaluation of women's character has led to their social exclusion in a two-fold sense: neither their intelligence nor their character was trusted. According to the Midrash, woman's lack of intelligence is even asserted in the Torah. This is derived from the passage in Exodus where Moses is told how to communicate the teaching to the Jewish people. The text reads: "Thus shall you speak to the house of Jacob and tell the children of Israel."[33] Undoubtedly there is a difference in meaning and emphasis between the Hebrew *tomar*, "to say, speak," and *tagged*, which connotes a more comprehensive and intense communication. At the same time, the phrase "the house of Jacob" is usually interpreted as referring to the women. The result is the following interpretation: "'Thus shall you speak to the house of Jacob'– these are

31. Rashi to Kiddushin 23b, s.v. *kinyan d'ishah.*
32. Menahot 43b.
33. Exodus 28:2.

the women. Give them *roshei devarim*, a short summary of the themes that they will be able to understand: 'And tell the children of Israel' – these are the men. They are to be taught the subjects in the minutest detail, for they are able to understand them.'[34] It is taken for granted that the intelligence of women is quite inferior to that of men; they are unable to study and to understand the Torah. Such an evaluation of female intelligence has, of course, certain halakhic consequences. Thus, for instance, the Talmud raises the following question: assume that a *get* (divorce document) is written on a tablet that belongs to the woman. According to the law, the material on which a *get* is written must be the property of the husband when he hands it to his wife to be divorced. In this case, the husband was giving this *get* to his wife. Since the material of the document has to be the husband's property, can we assume that the wife transferred possession of the material to the husband before he gave her the *get*, so that it became his property, or do we say: "His wife does not understand such a legal transaction"? Various attempts are made in order to prove that in similar cases of legal requirements, we assume that the necessary transfer is properly understood and executed. However, the proof is rejected. Says Rav Ashi, with a tone of indignation (note that a great part of the Talmud is verbal discussion between the teachers): "How can you cite that other case? Maybe it is different, for a man knows how to transfer possessions" (in a case like this). Also rejected is another example to prove that such a transfer may be assumed to have taken place, on the grounds that even an old man understands how to act in such a situation, but a woman may not have such understanding.[35] A similar example illustrates the same point. In Tractate *Kiddushin* the story is told of a man who gave a woman a piece of silk as the legal act of *kiddushin*, making her his wife.[36] In a case like this the object has to be appraised, for if it does not have the value declared by the husband, the *kiddushin* are invalid. What if the declared value is fifty and the piece of silk obviously is worth that much; is an official evaluation still necessary or not? Rabbah and Rav Joseph

34. Midrash Rabbah, Exodus 28:2.
35. Gittin 20b.
36. Kiddushin 7b.

disagree on this point. According to Rabbah no evaluation is necessary, for the indicated value is obvious. Not so Rav Joseph. He holds that the evaluation is still required; since women have no experience in evaluation, the woman in this case does not rely on the acknowledged value and is not really in agreement.

Not only did women not have the intelligence to understand more than an elementary introduction to a short summary of the subjects in the Torah, but according to Rabbi Eliezer, a father was forbidden to teach his daughter Torah.[37] The final conclusion thus was: "There is no other wisdom for a woman except at the spindle. As it is written: 'Every woman of wisdom of the heart was weaving with her hands.'"[38] One of the Midrashim defines women's status in one concise sentence that really says everything: "Women are incompetent to teach Torah [i.e., give decisions in accordance with Torah teaching], and one may not rely on their words." In essence this view introduces a new element into the evaluation of the female – lack of trust. One must not trust women. In a sense, this element appears, according to the explanation, in the reason that Rabbi Eliezer gives for not allowing a father to teach his daughter Torah. His words are: "He who teaches his daughter Torah teaches her lewdness." This is, of course, extremely disturbing, and the Talmud asks: "Lewdness? How can that be? Is the Torah lewdness?" The answer is: "Say it this way – it is as though he taught her lewdness." This correction reduces the astonishment somewhat, but still needs explanation. Rashi clarifies it as follows: "'As if'– because from her Torah studies she learns cunning and will do all kinds of things secretly."[39] This lack of trust has yet another significance: Women are not trusted in matters of possession.

We have learned that whatever a woman finds (*mezi'at haishah*) belongs to her husband. According to the Babylonian Talmud, the reason for this rule is to avoid possible hatred by the husband (or: to make her beloved by him – see above). The Jerusalem Talmud does give the same reason that is found in the Babylonian teaching. However

37. Sotah 20a.
38. Yoma 66b; citing Exodus 35:25.
39. Rashi on Sotah 1b.

immediately afterward follows the rather surprising and original opinion of Rabbi Yose, who said: "[Whatever the wife finds becomes the husband's property] so that she will not steal from her husband and say it is something she found."[40] Nothing could better express the significance of the midrashic statement quoted earlier that one may not rely on a woman's words. But obviously such an attitude toward a wife could not be limited to the case of found objects. It surely is due to a general, all-embracing suspicion.

Equally serious is the lack of trust regarding the woman's sexual behavior. It was generally accepted that women were more easily seduced than men. Thus, the Mishnah teaches: "A man should not isolate himself with two women, but two men may do so with one woman."[41] The explanation being: For women are light-minded (i.e., unreliable), and even two women in isolation with one man are easily seduced. Neither woman will be inhibited by the presence of the other, for each will readily act the same way. The situation is different with two men and one woman, in which case each man will be ashamed to commit an immoral act in the presence of the other.[42]

The lack of trust regarding sexual behavior led to limiting the woman's contact with male members of society. Maimonides sums up the social exclusion of women in these words:

> For every woman has the right to leave her home and go to her father's house in order to visit him or to a house of mourning or even to a wedding as an act of loving-kindness to her friend or relatives, so that they may also come and visit her. She is not like a prisoner that she should neither come nor go. But it is shameful for a woman to leave her home continually, at times outside her home and at others even walking in the streets. A husband should prevent his wife from doing this. He should not allow her to leave the house more than once in a month or twice, according to the need. For the beauty of a woman consists in her staying withdrawn in a corner of her home,

40. Yerushalmi, Ketubot, chap. 5.
41. Kiddushin 80b.
42. Rashi, ibid.

> for this is how it is written: "All the honor of the king's daughter is within [her home]."[43]

Maimonides here combines two elements of woman's seclusion: her husband's control over her and the affirmation of her dignity: the husband may not treat her as if she were a prisoner in his home, and she should appreciate that it is fitting for her to behave like a princess. However, a passage in the Talmud says that one of Eve's punishments was to be "kept in a prison." Rashi explains it by citing the very words quoted by Maimonides: "'A prison,' as it is written: All the honor of a king's daughter is within [her home]."[44]

Maimonides was most likely correct in ascribing the woman's secluded place in the home to "the dignity and honor of a king's daughter." Considering the social practices of his time, it was indeed not proper for a respectable woman to roam the streets and the marketplaces; it was improper and occasionally quite dangerous. Yet the seclusion of women was also a form of control exercised by their husbands that turned the home for them very nearly into a "prison." At least one midrashic opinion attempts to find a basis for such control in the Torah itself. When God created Adam, through him He blessed the future male race and said: "Multiply and fill the earth and subdue it."[45] If the word in the Hebrew original, *kivshuha*, were to stand by itself it may be understood as "subdue her," i.e., the woman. On it follows the explanation: "The man subdues [i.e., controls] his wife, so that she should not walk around the marketplaces [i.e., outside the home] and not fall into disgrace [or sin], as happened to Dinah, the daughter of Leah, the wife of Jacob."[46] For this reason she has to be kept back from public life. In Rabbi Meir's opinion, the generally accepted attitude towards the wife's withdrawal from society was: "She talks to her brothers and relatives and the husband does not object."[47]

43. Ishut 13:11, citing Psalms 45:14.
44. Eruvin 100b.
45. Genesis 1:28.
46. Genesis 34:1.
47. Gittin 90a.

A number of *halakhot* were based on the weakness of the female character in matters of sexual self-control. We have learned (see above) that if a woman brings into her marriage an appropriate number of maid-slaves who will do the work that she would otherwise be obligated to perform, she is free from those services. However, says Rabbi Eliezer: "Even if she brings with her a hundred servants, the husband has to compel her to do the work in wool-weaving, for idleness leads to lewdness."[48] It is worth nothing that immediately after this follows an opinion of Rabbi Simeon ben Gamliel, who says: "Even if the husband takes a vow regarding his wife that she should abstain from every kind of work [i.e., because of the 'nazirite oath' he imposes on her, she would not be permitted to do any kind of work as long as she is his wife], he has to divorce her and pay the value of her *ketubah*; for idleness leads to boredom." The opinion of Rabbi Simeon ben Gamliel shows a great concern for the woman that is altogether lacking in the attitude of Rabbi Eliezer. Yet, surprisingly, Maimonides cites the statement of Rabbi Simeon ben Gamliel as authoritative, but attaches to it the reasons given by Rabbi Eliezer – once again: for idleness leads to lewdness.

The nadir of the view of women's sexual conduct is reached in a statement by Resh Lakish. According to him a woman will, if need be, marry any man, "for it is better to dwell as two than to sit around like a widow." Added to this was the comment: "And all of them go and commit adultery, and the offspring is ascribed to the husband."[49]

4. OPINIONS

After all this, one should not be surprised by the many negative opinions about the nature of women. The Torah says: "And God built the rib He had taken from Adam as a woman."[50] One of the Talmudic teachers says:

48. Ketubot 59b.
49. Ibid. 72a.
50. Genesis 2:22.

> God has been considering from which part of Adam's body to build the woman. He decided: not from the head, she would carry herself proudly; not from the eye, that she not be inquisitive, prying; not from the ear, that she not be too submissive; and so on – none of these parts of the human body would come up to the divine expectations. Therefore, He decided on a place that is covered in man; even when a man stands naked, that place – of the ribs – is covered.[51]

In spite of it, all the divine fears about the negative character of the woman's personality came true. This is then illustrated by a number of examples found in the Bible itself. It is to this divine disappointment that Proverbs refers: "And they dissolved all my plans."[52] A similar statement about the female nature is found in another midrashic passage: "Our teachers said: 'Four qualities maintain women. They are gluttonous, docile, lazy, jealous.' Rabbi Judah ben Rabbi Nehemiah said: 'They are given to anger and are talkative.' Rabbi Levi said: 'They are also thievish and walk the streets.'"[53] Somewhat less critical is the saying: "Ten measures of talk was given to the world, of which women took nine, and one measure was left to the rest of the world."[54] More extreme is Rabbi Joshua's opinion that a woman prefers one measure of worldly goods and lewdness to nine measures of that which would impose continence on her.[55] In comparison to man, she was considered a poor hostess.[56]

5. TIME AND TORAH

If one considers the status of women as it emerges from these laws, mores, and opinions, one cannot help wondering: Is this Judaism?

51. Midrash Rabbah, citing Genesis 18:3.
52. Proverbs 1:25.
53. Midrash Rabbah, Genesis 45:48.
54. Kiddushin 49b.
55. Sotah 2a.
56. Bava Mezia 87a.

Is this Torah? How is all this reconciled with Torah values and ideals? What happened to "And thou shalt love your fellow as yourself?" and to "Righteousness, righteousness, thou shalt pursue"?

What's more, the record of women in the Torah is fundamentally different from what might be expected on the basis of this evaluation of them as human beings. To Abraham God says: "Whatever Sarah says to you, listen to her voice." It is Rebecca who sees Jacob's true worth, and not Isaac, who prefers Esau. In Egypt, Miriam acts as a prophetess beside Moses, and during the prophetic period there were prophetesses as well as prophets in Israel. Moreover, there were two outstanding female figures during the age of the "Shoftim" (Judges). Divine messages to ordinary people are sent through women. It is to the future mother that the angel is sent to foretell the birth of Samson and to teach her how to bring him up.[57] True, the rabbis maintain that her husband, Manoah, was an ignoramus in that he followed his wife's advice. But the fact is that it was the wife who received the "advice" and not the husband. Help is provided to the prophet Elijah by a woman chosen for this purpose by God. Similarly, Elisha, his successor in prophecy, was aided by a woman. In both cases, miracles of reviving a dead son were performed for the sake of the mothers.

The *nashim tzadkaniyot* ("righteous women") fulfilled a unique task in the history of the Jewish people. About the redemption from Egypt it is said that the Children of Israel were redeemed because of the merit of such women.[58] In the days of Ahasuerus, the Jews were saved through Esther; and at Hannukah, through Judith. There is even a general formulation to the effect that the Jewish people achieve redemption because of the *nashim tzadkaniyot* who live in their generation.[59] The only ones among the Children of Israel who refused to participate in the worship of the golden calf were the women. According to one tradition, they were given Rosh Hodesh as a reward to celebrate and observe as a Holy Day by not working.

It is noteworthy that whenever anyone challenged the rightness of a

57. Shoftim, chap. 13.
58. Pesahim 109b.
59. Midrash Zuta, Ruth.

law taught by Moses, it was women, not men, who did so. According to the biblical law of inheritance, only sons had the right to inherit the land of their fathers. This law had its justification. The promised land was to be distributed among the twelve tribes in proportion to their numbers. If women were to inherit with their brothers, it would happen, as a result of marriages of women of one tribe to men from other tribes, that the land would pass from tribe to tribe. This would upset the equity of the original division, by increasing the amount of land in some tribes and diminishing it in others. A man named Zelophehad died without male heirs so that the family remained without a share in the land. His daughters gathered courage "and stood before Moses, before the priest Eleazar, before the heads of the tribes and the entire people at the door of the tent of the sanctuary," and pleaded – giving the reasons for their pleading: "He died … leaving no sons; why should the name of our father be removed from the midst of his family because he has no son? Give us inheritance among our father's brothers!" When Moses brought the case before God for a decision, God said to him: "The daughters of Zelophehad speak rightly … give them their share in the inheritance of their father."[60]

It is remarkable that the rabbis, with similar great moral courage, elaborated the principle of justice that motivated the daughters. They assert that "when the daughters of Zelophehad heard that the land was to be distributed among the tribes but not to the female members, they assembled to consider the matter. They said: 'The loving-kindness of men of flesh and blood is unlike the loving-kindness of the Holy One, blessed be He: they prefer the male to the female human being; not so the Holy One, blessed be He; His loving-kindness is over all his works, as it is written, 'and His loving-kindness is over all his works.'"[61] And one cannot help wondering: did not the laws of inheritance established by Moses originate in the will of God? Did God have to be reminded that His loving-kindness was spread over all His works?

Finally, we hardly ever realize that to this day, religious Jews pray the daily *Shemoneh Esreh* in a manner which was taught us by Hannah, the

60. Numbers 27:2–6.
61. Sifrei, ibid., citing Psalms 145:9.

wife of Elkanah, who – in God's response to her prayer – became the mother of the prophet Samuel. Rabbi Hamnuna explains:

> How many important *halakhot* [laws of prayer] can we learn from what is said about Hannah's prayer: "And Hannah spoke from her heart"– this means that he who prays should concentrate in his heart; "only her lips moved" – he who prays should pronounce the words clearly; "and her voice was not heard" – this teaches us that it is forbidden to raise one's voice in one's prayers; "and Eli thought that she was drunk, etc." – this means that one must not pray when one is drunk.[62]

It is important to understand that the statements, laws, mores, and opinions that we have discussed thus far were not really about the nature of women, but about what women became as the result of the status granted them. Probably nothing proves this more clearly that the negative view about their intelligence.

We have quoted above the midrashic interpretation of the biblical words: "And God made a woman from Adam's rib." It held that God chose the rib after considering which part of Adam's body would be most suitable for the creation of Eve, but that His plans were ultimately defeated, because women have all the evil qualities that He wanted to eliminate (see above). However, surprisingly, there is also another interpretation of the word *va-yiven*, related to *binah*, "wisdom" – namely. that God provided Eve with wisdom, which teaches us that God gave woman understanding superior to that of man.[63] This has certain halakhic consequences. According to the law a person who takes an oath (e.g., to abstain from certain enjoyments) is required to keep it if he is mature enough to understand the meaning of the obligation that he imposed upon himself. Because of her superior intelligence, a girl at the age of twelve is adjudged to be capable of such understanding, while a boy reaches maturity at the age of thirteen. The Talmud adds: "This is the view of Rabbi [Rabbi Judah ha-Nasi, the editor of the Mishnah]."

62. Berakhot 31a, citing I Samuel 1:1.
63. Niddah 45b.

But Rabbi Simeon ben Elazar said: "What has been said about the young girl applies to the young boy, and *vice versa*: girls mature enough to obligate themselves should be of age thirteen."[64] The question, of course is: What happened to the female's superior intelligence? Tosafot explains that Rabbi Simeon ben Elazar does not disagree with Rabbi's original interpretation of the biblical *va-yiven*, but maintains that the boys' natural intelligence develops because he is so often in the house of his teacher, which is not the case for girls.

The opinion is formulated more explicitly in a midrash: "The way of a woman is to sit in her house; that of a man, to go out into the marketplaces, and thus he learns wisdom from other people."[65] What we understand here, then, is indeed, as Rabbi asserted, that women are by nature of superior intelligence, but that their intelligence cannot mature because of their lack of education, and exclusion from social and economic activities. They had no experience in legal matters, such as the legal forms of property transfer, or in monetary evaluation of everyday objects (see above). The failure to acknowledge the dignity of the female personality was also responsible for the lack of trust in monetary matters. As we saw, women had practically no rights in matters of property. The principle was: What a wife acquires belongs to her husband. There were some exceptions; for instance, the property a wife brought with her into her marriage (known as *nikhsei melog* and *nikhsei tzon barzel*), or property given her by others with the condition that her husband would have no right over it. But even with such property she did not have freedom of disposition, as the yields of it belong to her husband. Furthermore, if she died, the husband inherited her possessions; but when he died, she did not inherit from him (see above). No wonder, then, that occasionally a wife might be inclined to steal from her husband (see above).

Again, the necessity for laws obligating the wife to work in order to make herself beloved by her husband only underlies the impersonal character of a marriage that is based essentially on "arrangements." This is sufficient to explain the lack of trust in matters of sexual loyalty to

64. Ibid.
65. Genesis Rabbah 18a.

her husband. Everything was obligation, lacking the personal closeness and intimacy of love between husband and wife. Indeed, there could not have been much personal emotional commitment by the wife in a marriage in which the mutuality of personal intimacy was lacking. It is remarkable that, apparently, the Talmudic teachers were themselves aware of the basic impersonality of such marriages. Among the "curses" bestowed on Eve and, through her, on women in general is one that "she was [as if] ostracized from all men." The explanation is that whereas a husband may marry as many women as he pleases, without consideration for his wife's feelings, a woman must not marry more than one husband.[66]

Some of the Talmudic statements most objectionable in our times are indeed not about women, but what the society in which they lived made of them. We noted Resh Lakish's opinion that a woman would be willing to marry any man because it is better to live with anyone rather than be unmarried; but then she would go and commit adultery and say that the offspring was her husband's. In a society in which women had no education or profession and in all matters of maintenance were completely dependent on their husbands, such behavior on the part of women is understandable. In a similar manner, one may also understand the law (see above) that one must not relieve one's wife of any of the services a woman is obligated to perform, for such freedom would lead to *tiflut* (immorality, lewdness). Indeed, in a society in which a woman must stay secluded in her home, how could she endure idleness? Opinions and laws of this kind bespeak the nature of the society rather than essential female character.

In a sense, the same applies to what may be considered the most radically negative statement about female behavior. We are referring to witchcraft. In the Torah itself we find the verse: "Let not a witch live." The Talmud explains: "Why is a female witch mentioned [the Hebrew for 'witch,' *mekhashefah*, is feminine]? Because mostly women engage in witchcraft."[67] Is this really true? Does the Torah say so? It is a personal opinion, and it must have some timely basis. In the Ethics of the Fathers,

66. Eruvin 100b.
67. Sanhedrin 67b.

it is said: "He who marries many wives increases witchcraft." Finally, we hear the opinion: "The best among women engage in witchcraft."[68] Perhaps this final opinion qualifies all the previous statements and also offers an explanation. Obviously, most women are not "the best" among women. Why, indeed, would the best among women be engaged in witchcraft? It seems to us that this too tells more about the society than about the nature of women. Who would be "the best among women" referred to in this context? Clearly, not the most pious, the most modest and observant. By "the best among women" are meant those who are most intellectually gifted and energetic; those who would be, if permitted, the most able to prove themselves and assert their personal dignity. For this very reason, they are the most frustrated women in a society in which females have no education, and are denied any form of active participation in the life of the community aside from "bringing their children to the Talmud Torah"[69] and waiting for their husbands until they return from the house of study. It is understandable that many of them turned to the dark realm of witchcraft, where their gifts and capabilities could find a form of fulfillment. One might see in this a form of rebellious self-affirmation. It may be that the example set by the "best of women" influenced many less-gifted women, who then followed their example. That would explain the view of Rabbi Simeon ben Yohai, who noted that in "later generations, the daughters of Israel do not keep themselves from witchcraft activities."[70] This may have been an unconscious rebellion of sorts against the treatment women received.

In attempting to understand this strange phenomenon in Jewish life, we must realize that many of the negative opinions about women and their place in society are not authentically Jewish. For instance, a study of the practices in classical Greece reveals many similarities and parallels between the two societies. For example, the established principle was "that men are born to rule and women to obey." The treatment of wives followed this principle. Socrates, for instance, when he was dying, desired to be among his male friends. His wife, Xanthippe, he dismissed

68. Sotah 15b.
69. Berakhot 17a.
70. Eruvin 64b.

bluntly from his deathbed. This, in itself, was a dramatic indication of the emotional gulf between husband and wife. The purpose of marriage was procreation, and woman is occasionally referred to as a "field to plow." In fact, "since the male seed is all-important, any female will do." In Aeschylus' *Eumenides* the mother's role in conception is described as totally passive, "a receptacle for the father's seed." Thus, it follows that the mother is not a parent but only a nurse "to the newly sown embryo." The impersonality of the husband-wife relationship in marriage is determined by the woman's complete lack of social independence, which is described in the following terms:

> Citizen women were perpetually under the guardianship of a man, usually the father or, if he were dead, the male next-of-kin. Upon marriage the woman passed into the guardianship of her husband in most matters, with the important limitation that her father, or whoever else had given her in marriage, retained the right to dissolve the marriage. If the husband predeceased the wife, the guardianship of her dowry, and perhaps of her person, passed to her sons if they were of age, or to their guardians.

The separation of women from men was like a replica of what we found in early Jewish society. There were separate quarters for men and women. "Free women were usually secluded so that they could not be seen by men who were not close relatives." It was maintained "that some women were even too modest to be seen by men who were relatives, and for a strange man to intrude upon free women in the house of another man was tantamount to a criminal act." Men spent most of their time in public areas, such as the marketplace, etc. Respectable women remained at home. Greek women would sit secluded in the interior parts of the house.

The work of the Greek wife was not different from that of her Jewish counterpart. The housework was entirely her responsibility. If the house was wealthy, she supervised the work of the slaves. However, working in wool was traditionally a woman's task. "When Augustus wished to instill respect for old-fashioned virtues among the sophisticated women of his household, he set them to work in wool and wore their homespun results."

(One is, of course, reminded of the Talmudic statement that the only wisdom of women is in the spindle.)

As for women's intelligence, Aristotle, to cite one example, taught that "the deliberative part of a woman's soul was impotent and needed supervision," whereas his disciple, Theophrastus, maintained "that more education would turn women into rather lazy, talkative busybodies." These ideas about the education of women recall Maimonides' interpretation of Rabbi Eliezer's statement as to why a father should not teach his daughter Torah (see above): "Our sages commanded that one should not teach one's daughter Torah because the minds of most women are incapable of concentrating on learning, and thus, because of their intellectual poverty, they turn the words of the Torah into words of nonsense – vain talk."[71] The handling of property was also determined by woman's limited intelligence. "Women in Greece could acquire property through their dowries, or by inheritance as sisters, cousins, nieces, and aunts… Some women were actively aware of financial matters, but their property was nevertheless managed by male guardians." Greek women did not even go to market for food. Purchase and exchange were considered financial transactions too complicated for women to be entrusted with. There was also the additional desire to "protect women from the eyes of strangers and intimate dealings with shop keepers."[72]

We shall conclude this section of our study with two quotations. In the Talmud and Midrash we find a discussion of the apparent contradiction between Proverbs 18:22, "One who has found a wife finds goodness," and Ecclesiastes 7:26, "I find the wife to be more bitter than death itself." The contradiction is resolved by the explanation: "If she is a good wife, there is no end to her goodness; if she is a bad wife, there is no end to her badness."[73] The Greek poet Hesiod said much the same thing: "A man wins nothing better than a good wife and nothing worse than a bad one."[74]

71. Talmud Torah 1:13.

72. The material presented here on the status of women in classical Greece is all from Sarah P. Pomeroy, *Goddesses, Whores, Wives, and Slaves: Women in Classical Antiquity.*

73. Yevamot 63b; Midrash Shoher Tov, chap. 59.

74. Quoted by Pomeroy, op. cit., p. 48.

One is almost inclined to ask whether Hesiod was influenced by the Midrash or whether the Midrash was aware of Hesiod's formulation. However, the question should be asked in its widest application. In view of the similarities between the ancient Jewish and ancient Greek societies, there is no need for us to enter into detailed historical research as to dates and possible contacts. It is quite clear that we are here confronted with a general, purely human phenomenon. Obviously, this is how women were evaluated in the original male-established social structure. Their status was determined in accordance with the functions they were able to perform in such societies. These were matters completely time-conditioned and subject to the values entertained and understood by the men and women of the period. The original forms of social and economic life upon which the status of women was based were not introduced and established by the Torah.

The social, economic, and even religious practices of early Jewish society were sometimes contrary to principles of the Torah. But how could Judaism make peace with them? How could it live with them? This question introduces us to one of the major problems of Halakhah.

The Torah addresses itself to man in this world. As is emphasized in the Talmud, the Torah was not given to God-serving angels. The task is to improve the world by the ideal of divine kingship, i.e., by the acknowledgment of divine authority. But the world is this world. It is the raw material of which man himself is a part. In this respect, Jews share their human nature with the rest of mankind. The Torah speaks to man. But to which man? The words of eternity are addressed to man in time, to man who is forever changing as the times change. How can the same teaching meaningfully be conveyed to the Jew at the time of the Exodus, then again during the First and Second Temples? Can we expect the same values to be appreciated by the Jews of Babylon and hundreds of years later by Spanish Jewry? Can the goals and aspirations of Judaism in the Middle Ages be shared by the Jewries of the Modern Age? And yet God speaks the same word to all generations. How is that possible? How may the word of eternity function meaningfully in the midst of the earthly reality of time-conditioned human beings?

It would seem that the rabbis of the Midrash dealt with one aspect of the problem. One need not call on the changing times in order to formulate the issue. In every society, at any time, people differ in their physical capacities and intellectual abilities, in their imagination, tastes, desires, and goals for life. Yet there seems to be one and the same truth for all.

Commenting on Psalms 29:4, "The voice of God [came] with power," Rashi says: "At the time of the giving of the Torah, God limited His voice in accordance with the strength of the Israelites to receive." The thought is developed with greater clarity in the Midrash on Exodus. It is noted that the psalmist does not say that the voice of God was heard "with His power" but simply "with power." The meaning is that standing at Sinai, each one received the Voice in accordance with his own strength: the old people in accordance with their strength, and so also the young ones, the children, and the women – each group heard it commensurate with its own strength. It is true that the reference here is to physical capacity. Had God spoken to them with the might of His strength, no one could have endured it. Each received the Voice at a pitch appropriate to his or her hearing capacity. But if this was true of the physical quality of the Voice, how much more is it evident that they all received the same word, but each in conformity with his own spiritual and moral capacity. There is no other way of receiving the meaning of any communication.

Maimonides was fully aware of the consequences of this human condition. His solution of the problem may be learned from his interpretation of the animal sacrifices the Jewish people were commanded to offer in the Sanctuary of Jerusalem. According to Maimonides, prayer is a form of divine service far superior to animal sacrifices. That being so, why were they not ordered from the very beginning to pray rather than bring *korbanot*? This is his explanation:

> It is impossible for man to change suddenly from one extreme to the other. It is impossible for him suddenly to give up what he has been accustomed to. As God sent Moses to make us "a kingdom of priests and a holy nation,"[75] and to dedicate ourselves to His service, as it is

75. Exodus 9:6.

> said: "And to serve Him with all your heart"[76], the prevailing custom in the world was to sacrifice animals in the temples which people had erected to their idols, to bow down to them and burn incense before them, etc. God's wisdom counseled Him that to command the Jews to give up all that kind of service and annul it completely would have been something that their hearts could not have accepted. Human nature is forever inclined towards the accustomed practice. Such a command would be as if a prophet came to us [today] to call us to the service of God and said: "God has commanded you not to pray to Him or fast or ask for help in times of trouble, but to make your service be pure thought without any action." [In fact, this is what Maimonides considered the *avodah aharonah*, the ultimate service of God by pure thought meditating upon Him.] For this reason, God allowed the [generally practiced] sacrificial services to remain, but directed them away from those created or imagined powers, in which there is no truth, to His own name, blessed be He, and commanded to dedicate them to Him. Thus, He commanded us to build a sanctuary to Him, etc., and that the sacrifices shall be offered to Him: "If one from among you will offer a sacrifice unto Me,"[77] etc. Thus, this divine guidance achieved its purpose - that even the memory of idol worship was erased among us, and the important truth was established in the midst of our people, i.e., the existence of God and His unity.[78]

The goal has been set, "to serve Him with all your heart," which the rabbis explained as follows: "What is the service of the heart? It is prayer." Yet this goal was to be achieved only gradually, by a guided change in the human capacity to understand and absorb it. Numerous authorities do not agree with Maimonides' interpretation of the meaning of animal sacrifices. But the principle that he uses for his interpretation has general validity and reveals Judaism's basic method for the application of the eternal word of God to the time-conditioned reality of the human situation.

76. Deuteronomy 11:13.
77. Leviticus 1:2.
78. *Moreh Nevukhim* 3:32.

It says: The goals and the values are these forever. But they are taught and applied with the wisdom of understanding that time-conditioned reality cannot be changed overnight. The method of the Torah is to acknowledge reality, to take human nature into account and apply the eternal word to it so far as is possible, thus to teach values and guide behavior, indicating the goal towards which the guided change has to move. The goal is to integrate the eternal with the temporal; not to change human nature but to realize its potential. This is the principle that one may derive from Maimonides' interpretation of the meaning of animal sacrifices in the Temple of Jerusalem. Whether one agrees with his interpretation in this specific case or not, the principle as such has general validity. Maimonides rightly maintains that one may find many examples of this kind of guidance in the Torah.

We shall consider here just one case, that of slavery. It is not our intention to consider it in its general significance. Judaism's attitude to the Canaanite slave requires a special study, but the ideal is fully indicated in the words of Job, who says: "Do I deny justice to my slave, male or female, when they quarrel with me? And what would I do when God arose and recalled it? How could I answer Him? Did not the One who formed him form me, too, and shape us in one womb?"[79] Even regarding the Canaanite slave, the teaching was:

> Notwithstanding the law, the qualities of piety and wisdom require that one be merciful and pursue justice and not impose one's yoke on one's slave. One should not oppress him and should give him to eat and drink from all available food and drink [i.e., the same as one's own food and drink]. The sons of our father Abraham – the Jews, upon whom the Holy One, blessed be He, poured out in abundance the good that is the Torah, and commanded them just statutes and laws – have mercy on all. Such are the attributes of the Holy One, blessed be He, that they [the Jewish people] are commanded to imitate, which declare that His mercies are on all His works. To the one who is merciful, mercy is granted, as it is said:

79. Job 31:13–14.

"And He will treat you with mercy and will increase you."[80]

It is remarkable that even between Jew and Jew, slavery was not excluded. How was the principle of gradual guidance toward the realization of a common brotherhood implemented? Right from the beginning there were radical changes from what was general practice in other civilizations. In biblical times, a thief who could not return what he had stolen or pay for its value would be sold as a slave through a rabbinical court. However, he could only be sold for a term of six years. At any time during his enslavement, if he came into the possession of funds sufficient to pay his master the sum he had paid for him, minus the value of the time he had already served, he was permitted to do so and go free. In general, he was to be treated like a hired servant, not like a slave; thus, he was freed from certain kinds of labor that were usually done by slaves, such as carrying his master's change of clothing to the bath and taking off his master's shoes. The master had to treat him like an equal in matters of food, drink, clothing, and living conditions ("for he should have it good with you").[81] When the years of his slavery were up, the Jewish slave was not to be sent away emptyhanded. He was to be paid a "severance fee," probably the first ever in human history, as it is written: "You should grant him from your sheep, your barn, and your wine cellar. You should give him from that with which God has blessed you."[82] In general, slaves were to be treated with respect, as befit fellow Israelites. As a result of all this, Jews eventually concluded that he who bought himself a slave bought himself a master.[83] Far be it from me to maintain that Jews always followed these rules and teachings. There is sufficient proof in the Torah to the contrary. Yet there is little doubt in my mind that in a Jewish state, governed by these teaching and rules, had it been in existence, slavery would have been abolished long centuries before the age of Lincoln.

In the case of slavery, Judaism was confronted with the same problem

80. Maimonides, Hilkhot Avadim, conclusion, citing Deuteronomy 13:18.
81. Leviticus 25:40.
82. Deuteronomy 15:14.
83. Kiddushin 20a.

that Maimonides discusses with regard to animal sacrifices. International historical experience in this matter is more than sufficient to prove that a biblical command to forbid slavery would not have been understood and would certainly not have been accepted. On the contrary, it would have led to an active rejection of the ideas of respect for human dignity and equality of status before God. The method used was guided by the ideal, which was applied effectively to the time-conditioned situation.

This, indeed, is the essential nature of Halakhah: It recognizes the continually changing human condition. Its task is not to change the law as man and conditions change. That would not be Torah-guidance. Halakhah affirms the law, but – recognizing the ultimate authority of the word of God as revealed in the Torah – applies it in a manner that enables the meaning and purpose of the law to guide man and society in the context of the aimed-at integration of Torah and life. Judaism commits the Jew to the ever-enduring vital partnership with God. The result is *Torat Hayyim*, a living Torah.

6. TORAH-TOLERATED, NOT TORAH-TAUGHT

Undoubtedly, the basic views and values that originally determined the status of women in Jewish society were not derived from the Torah, even though many of them were later given midrashic justification. They were Torah-tolerated because they could not be abolished with an act of Torah legislation. They had to be tolerated, but certain changes and differences were present which indicated that an entirely different system of values and teachings also existed. The most significant difference between ancient Greece and early Jewish society is to be seen in the fact that in the latter women were not under guardians. The father was the guardian of his minor daughter (as we shall see, his guardianship was limited). But once she came of age, at twelve years and six months, she could not be given into marriage against her will. It is indeed true that once she was married she came under the authority of her husband; but as we saw above, while a Greek woman returned to the guardianship of her father (or her nearest male relative, if the father had died) after a divorce, a divorced Jewish woman remained free and under her own control. While a Jewish woman's marriage could only be dissolved by her husband, even this may be better appreciated when one compares it with the Greek guardian's power over his ward, for he could dissolve her marriage at any time, even against her will. This had far-reaching consequences. A marriage that can be revoked at any time by an outsider does not confer the same sense of permanence offered by a marriage which is completely handed over into the care of a personal relationship between husband and wife. A marriage that can be annulled at any time by outside interference cannot develop the same sense of personal closeness, nor does it allow the same strength of mutual moral commitment, as the one whose quality of worth depends completely upon a mutuality of understanding between husband and wife. Thus, Judaism's abolition of continuous guardianship over women was in itself a revolutionary change in their social status. It meant a recognition of their maturity and gave them a measure of responsibility for the management of their personal lives. It was an indication of the course to be followed in the movement towards a more just recognition of the female personality.

The fact that the negative opinions about Jewish women were not unanimous indicates that there was another source determining woman's status. Much was Torah-tolerated, but there was also Torah-guidance. We have already considered the interpretation of the biblical words that God made the woman from one of Adam's ribs. This took place after God weighed the evil consequences that would follow if any other part of the male body were used for the purpose. Yet it was all to no avail. The feared evil materialized in the woman. God's plan was defeated. As we learned, the same words were also interpreted as indicating that God gave women a greater measure of understanding than men. True, as we also saw, because of the social conditions, women had no chance to develop their intellectual potential. But the idea that feminine intellect was by its nature superior to that of the male indicates a certain human dignity whose actualization was denied to women by the man-made status allowed to them.

There are also other considerable disagreements between the Talmudic teachers about the nature of women. Relying on the prophet Isaiah's criticism of the public behavior of the daughters of Israel in his day, there is an opinion that describes their very walking as overbearing, seductive pride.[84] On the other hand, in the Midrash Tanhuma it is said: "The daughters of Israel are not loud, neither do they walk proudly and do not break out in hilarity."[85] They are modest in their behavior. Or as it is also put: "The daughters of Israel are pleasant."[86] According to the Jerusalem Talmud, it is not the way of women to be lazy.[87] There is a world of difference between this appreciation and the insultingly negative opinions, cited above, that describe women as gluttonous, docile, lazy, and curious, and according to Rabbi Judah, as "given to anger, uncontrolled and talkative"[88] as well. How different is the evaluation that describes women as merciful.[89] We have opinions that women are more ungenerous towards guests than men.[90] But Rabbi Yosi bar Hanina, basing himself on the words of the Shunammite woman, who said to her husband about Elisha, "Behold, please, I have known that he is a God-dedicated, saintly man," explains: "This shows that a woman has more sensitivity in recognizing a guest than a man."[91] We find the same view stated in simpler language: "The woman acknowledges a guest more readily than the man."[92] As for the rule of woman's unreliability, it could not be consistently applied. The first Mishnah in the tractate of Hullin starts with the words: All may perform the religious slaughter of animals [i.e., *shehitah*], and their performance is kosher [i.e., in conformity with the required laws]." The Talmud explains that most people who occupy themselves with *shehitah* are reliable. Of course, the Mishnah's statement that the *shehitah* of all is acceptable includes women. The Tosafot, commenting on this Mishnah, quotes the *Hilkhot Eretz Yisrael*, which states that women should not do religious slaughtering because they are "lightminded," i.e., emotionally

84. Shabbat.
85. Nasso.
86. Nedarim 82–89, Niddah 36.
87. Ketubot 5:6.
88. Midrash Genesis Rabbah 45:46.
89. Megillah 18b.
90. Bava Mezia 87.
91. Midrash Rabbah 10, citing II Kings 4:9.
92. Berakhot 10a.

unable to endure the act of slaughter. However, relying on what is said in Tractate Zevahim,[93] Tosafot maintains that the author of *Hilkhot Eretz Yisrael* was only expressing his personal opinion. Tosafot and many other leading authorities reject this opinion.[94] Nevertheless, the custom developed that women are not permitted to perform *shehitah*. There were arguments as to whether the custom (*minhag*) may, in this case, invalidate the halakhah (law).[95] It is remarkable that even the insistence on the power of the *minhag* could not be consistently upheld. In another context the question arises as to why we can rely on the testimony of only one woman that the meat that she serves in her home is kosher. The answer given is based on the principle that the testimony of one witness, which normally would not be relied on, is admitted if the matter on which the witness testifies is *be-yado*, i.e., in his power to perform. Tosafot remarks that since a woman can learn how to carry out the ritual of slaughtering, the matter is *be-yadah*, in her power. She is therefore trusted.[96] Obviously, in the widest sense of the word the custom of not allowing a woman to do *shehitah* became baseless.

In a similar sense, the obligation of a woman to do every kind of housework and also serve her husband (see above) was not strictly observed. First of all, there is a dissenting opinion. Referring to the Mishnah listing the manifold duties of the wife, it is said: "This is not in accordance with the opinion of Rabbi Hiyya, who insisted: 'A wife is only for beauty and for the sake of children.' Rabbi Hiyya also taught that he who wishes his wife to be delicate should clothe her in fine linen."[97] But even according to the opinion that all the housework is a woman's obligation, Maimonides, basing himself on the Talmud, states: "Everything is to be done in accordance with the custom of the land. If it is not customary for women to do those jobs, one cannot force them to carry them out." Similarly, the Rosh, a great halakhic authority, quotes a halakhic decision that "now, in our days, it is not the way of

93. Zevahim 31b.
94. *Tur*, Yoreh Deah 1.
95. Ibid.
96. Gittin 3b, Tosafot.
97. Ketubot 59b.

women to mill, and to do laundry; they cannot be compelled to do such work." The Rosh was born in 1250 and died in 1328. It is difficult to say when the practice he cites, the freeing of women from certain onerous jobs, came into existence. However, we find in the Talmud that the women in the city of Mehoza did not mill or do laundry. The custom of the women in Mehoza is significant. However, in both of the cases quoted above, the opinion of Rabbi Hiyya and that of Maimonides, where such work is not customary, it is emphasized that the women were required to weave.[98] These are comments added to the text by the commentators. There is little doubt that the women of the Middle Ages were legally free from all kinds of housework, including weaving. It is very likely that this was also in accord with the halakhic decision quoted by the Rosh.[99]

98. On Rabbi Hiyya, see Tosafot, ibid.; for Maimonides, see Ishut 21.
99. Pesahim 20b.

II Woman as a Person

"For thou art a holy nation to the Eternal One, your God." Rabbi Elwazar explained, "Men as well as women." (Yerushalmi, Kiddushim 1, 7)

1. TORAH IDEALS AND TEACHING

The examples discussed in the previous chapter are an indication that the aspect of the wife's duties that brought her status closest to that of a servant was gradually disregarded. The more positive and appreciative opinions and practices undoubtedly indicate that woman's status gradually changed to something far different from the more primitive position granted her in the original man-made and man-dominated society. We are no longer dealing with an early, unavoidably Torah-tolerated status, but with a transformation to a Torah-directed, Torah-required status based on Torah teaching. The teaching represents a radical rejection of the original male-determined and male-dominated position of women.

We shall quote some of the principles of the teaching. Rabbi Eleazar said: "Any man who has no wife is not a man, for it says in the Torah: 'Male and female He created them and called their name Adam.'"[1] Man and woman together are a complete Adam. Rabbi Helbo said: "One should always be especially careful [to safeguard] the honor of one's wife, for the blessing in one's house is found only by the merit of one's wife." About honoring one's wife it is also said: "He who loves his wife as himself and honors her more than himself – of him does the

1. Yevamot 63a, citing Genesis 3:2.

Torah say, 'and you will know that there is peace in your home, etc.'"[2] In the same context, we also find the saying: "He who has no wife lives without joy, without blessing, without the goodness of life, [and finally] without life." This statement assumes that the wife is treated as expressed in the previous sayings. According to the Jerusalem Talmud, on the occasion of one's marriage all one's sins are forgiven.[3] In the same vein Rabbi Alexander taught: "Anyone whose wife dies during his life, the world itself is darkened for him."[4] Rav Samuel ben Nahman said: "Everything can be replaced; but for the wife of one's youth there is no replacement." It was also taught: "A man dies only for his wife; and a woman, only for her husband."[5] It was further taught: "A person whose wife dies is forbidden to remarry until the passing of three festivals, so that he will be without any joy during that period and will not forget the love of his wife."[6] For all these teachings proofs are quoted from verses in the Torah.

The evaluation of the woman's importance has significant halakhic consequences. We may start with the halakhic determination of certain questions pertaining to the wife's obligations. If a wife refuses a husband's request that she nurse her child, and it is her family's custom not to breast-feed, we rule in her favor. However, what is the law when it is her way to breast-feed but not so in his family? After whose custom is one to decide? For the decision that according to her husband's wont she is free from this obligation, two reasons are given. First, by her marriage she rises to the social and material status of her husband, but never descends from her own status. This principle is based on the midrashic interpretation of two words in the Torah that describe the status of a married woman – *be'ulat ba'al*,[7] which is interpreted in this way. Second, according to Rabbi Eleazar, the decision is based on the biblical words about the nature of Eve, of whom it is said that "she was the mother of all the living" (i.e., all human beings). The words mean that the woman

2. Yevamot 62b.
3. Bikkurim 1:5.
4. Menahot 22.
5. Ibid., 22b.
6. Tosafot to Mo'ed Katan 23a.
7. Genesis 20:3.

was given "for life and not for suffering."[8] There is little doubt that these reasons, which qualify and limit the wife's original obligation, are a breakthrough towards a new determination of the woman's status. For instance, the principle that a wife rises to her husband's status obliges him to maintain her according to his financial capacity.[9] Whereas it was originally said that preserving the man's life takes precedence over preserving the woman's, it was later determined that if a man dies, and the possessions he leaves are sufficient for his sons and daughters, the sons become the heirs and the daughters are supported from the father's possessions. If the possessions are not sufficient for both the sons and the daughters, however, then the daughters are the ones that inherit and the sons have to support themselves by begging.[10] In the same spirit it was declared that if two orphans, one a male and the other a female, have to be supported by charity funds, the female orphan is to be provided for first, and the male only afterwards; because it is the way of a man to go begging, but it is not the way of a woman to do so. The same preference is given to the female orphan when two orphans have to be married off. The female is married off first, and then the male, since a woman feels more shame at being unmarried than does a man.[11] There is one halakhah in which these two earlier principles are disregarded. We have quoted the law that if a son's father and mother both ask him for a glass of water, he has to offer it to his father first, then to his mother; for he and his mother both have the duty to honor the father. The halakhah we will quote seems to overrule this law as the one that, in matters of sustenance, the male is to be given preference over the woman. According to Tractate Horayot,[12] if a person is in captivity together with his father and his Torah teacher, and all three need to be ransomed, then he comes before his teacher, and his teacher before his father. But if his mother is also held captive, then she is to be given preference over all of them. Surely, in captivity, the danger to the

8. Ketubot 61a.
9. E.g., Maimonides, Ishut 11:12.
10. Bava Batra 139b.
11. Ketubot 67b.
12. Fol. 13.

woman is more serious than the danger to the men, but if sustaining a male alive is our duty, this would seem all the more reason to ransom the male captive before the female. Similarly, if we must honor a father by handing him a glass of water first, how much more important would it be to honor him by giving him preference over the mother where his life might be in jeopardy! Clearly, this reflects Judaism as taught and prescribed, and not just Judaism in its toleration of ancient customs.

One may judge the status of women as mothers by the following examples. When Rabbi Judah ha-Nasi, the editor of the Mishnah, sensed that his death was approaching, he said: "I need my sons." When his sons entered, he said to them: "Take extreme care regarding the honor of your mother."[13] Of Rabbi Joseph it is told that when he heard the footsteps of his mother, he said: "I shall stand before the Shekhinah [divine presence] that has arrived."[14]

2. HALAKHIC INNOVATIONS

The halakhic consequences of this teaching were revolutionary and far-reaching. According to Torah law, a father has the power to give his minor daughter (up to the age of twelve years and six months) in marriage to whomever he pleases. But the Rabbis taught that it is not right to do so, and commanded that the father wait until the child is mature enough to say: "This is the one I wish to marry." Tosafot explains that because of the uncertainties of a *galut* existence we cannot afford to wait until our daughters are of age to marry, since we may not be able to provide their dowries at that time.[15] This comment is significant because it also explains the reason for the original law. The father was permitted to give a minor daughter in marriage because conditions were such that a female child obtained a degree of protection through marriage that she would not have in the home of her parents. For a

13. Ketubot 103a.

14. Kiddushin 31a.

15. Tosafot, Kiddushin 41a, s.v. *keshehi*; for the ruling in the case of the father's death, see, e.g., Yevamot 107b.

very similar reason the rule was later established that in the event of the father's death, his authority in this matter passes to the child's mother and brothers.

Legally, a man has the right to appoint a representative to act for him in performing the marriage ceremony of *Kiddushin*. Rav, one of the leading Talmud teachers in Babylon, ruled that one must not do so unless previously acquainted with the intended bride. One should not do so because it is written: "And thou shalt love your neighbor as yourself." Without having previously known the bride, he might find that he would be unable to love her.[16] The same command of the Torah is also used in order to forbid sexual relations between husband and wife in the daylight, for in the light of day the husband might discover bodily blemishes on his wife that would estrange him from her.[17]

Rules were introduced in order to limit the power of the husband over his wife. Legally a husband had the right to divorce his wife whenever it pleased him to do so. In order to curb the willfulness of husbands, the *ketubah* (marriage contract) was introduced. It requires that a husband who wants to divorce his wife must pay her two hundred silver coins, a sum not readily available to most husbands. According to the accepted Talmudic view, the *ketubah* was instituted so that "it shall not be easy in his eyes [i.e., the husband's] to divorce her."[18] A similar restriction was also placed on the grounds for divorce. In the Mishnah we find that Bet Hillel and Rabbi Akiva offer rather surprising explanations to justify a husband's divorcing his wife. According to the House of Hillel, the husband may divorce her if "she has burnt his food." Rabbi Akiva maintains that the husband's finding another woman "more pleasing" is sufficient reason for a divorce. Strangely enough, both teachers find proof for these opinions in the Torah itself. One may take comfort from the fact that Bet Shammai interprets the relevant biblical passage as saying that "a husband should not divorce his wife unless he finds her violating sexual morality."[19] It is important to note that even though

16. Kiddushin 41a.
17. Niddah 17a.
18. Kiddushin 11a.
19. Gittin 90a.

the opinions of Bet Hillel are usually accepted as valid as against the teaching of Bet Shammai, in this case the Halakhah is according to Bet Shammai.[20]

Even more remarkable are the halakhic innovations that were introduced in order to protect the wife from becoming an *agunah*, i.e., a woman not divorced and thus bound to her husband and yet in fact having no husband to live with. We shall list a number of such cases. According to the law of the Torah, the husband is required to pay the scribe for writing the *get* (divorce document). Referring to the Mishnah, the Gemara explains: "However, these days we do not do it that way. The rabbis have 'thrown this obligation upon the wife [i.e., she has to pay the scribe], to make sure that he [the husband] does not abandon her because he refuses to pay for the writing of the divorce document."[21] How serious a matter this was may be judged from the words of Rabbi Hisda, who said: "I really could invalidate all the *gittin*."[22] Since he does not give any reason for this statement, the possibility is discussed that he would do so because it was not the husband who had paid for the writing of the *get* but the wife. This idea is rejected on the grounds of the principle of *hefker bet din hefker*; i.e., if the authorized rabbinical court expropriates someone's property, it becomes *hefker* (ownerless), and anyone may take possession of it. Thus, the money that the wife pays is as if the husband himself had paid it. This is done in the vital interest of the wife.[23] After some time, the original biblical law was restored and the husband had to pay the fee to the scribe.[24]

Even more radical were the innovations in matters of testimony. According to the Mishnah, when witnesses to a divorce are unable to read, one reads the *get* to them and then they sign it. Similarly, when the witnesses cannot sign their names, one outlines the letters of their names on clean paper, and they fill in the outlines with ink. Adds Rabban Simeon ben Gamliel: "Only in regard to the divorce document

20. Maimonides, Gerushin 2:27.
21. Bava Batra 167a.
22. Gittin 20a.
23. Ibid.
24. See Magid Mishnah, Gerushin 2:4.

are such practices permitted, but in all other kinds of documents, only witnesses who are able to read and write are accepted to testify." Rabbi Eleazar explains that the testimony of illiterate witnesses was allowed so that the daughters of Israel would not become *agunot*. The reason, of course, is that a husband in a hurry to leave his domicile, for some reason or other, and unable to find a fully qualified witness, may simply abandon his wife without a divorce.[25]

Numerous other halakhic deviations from some of the basic laws of the Torah were introduced in order to prevent women from becoming *agunot*. Apparently, divorces occurred so often that scribes would keep a supply of the general impersonal text of a *get* on hand for immediate use when needed. The Mishnah declared that scribes who did so must leave place for the husband's name, the wife's name, and the time of the anticipated divorce until the *get* was actually requested by the husband.[26] The Talmud adds that this was because the Torah says: ""He should write it [the *get*] for her"; the husband has to arrange the writing of the *get*, addressed to his wife's name.[27] This, however, requires further explanation. There are two entirely divergent opinions for the significance of the testimony. Rabbi Meir teaches that the signatures of the witnesses are decisive for the divorce, whereas Rabbi Eliezer maintains that the witnesses' testimony that the *get* was actually handed to the wife establishes its validity. According to Rabbi Meir, even the *toref*, the essential part of the *get*, with the names of the parties and the time, could be written in advance, since the witnesses only testify to their signatures. But why was it ruled that the *toref* part of the *get* could not be prepared in advance? Because there may occasionally be a quarrel between husband and wife, and if *gittin* are too easily available, and required only the signatures of the two witnesses to be valid, the husband, in his anger, may hastily divorce his wife. According to Rabbi Eliezer, even the nonessential part of the *get* should not be prepared in advance. The witnesses' testimony to the handing over of the entire document is decisive; but if the text was written in advance, it was not

25. Gittin 19b.
26. Ibid. 26a.
27. Ibid. 26b.

handed over specifically to the wife. Nevertheless, it was permitted to prepare the *toref* in advance, for it might happen that the husband might be in a hurry to leave, and if it was difficult to find a scribe immediately, he would leave her without a divorce and she would be an *agunah*.

Great leniency was practiced in the case of testimony about the death of a husband. According to the Halakhah, a fact is established if two witnesses attest to it from their own personal knowledge and not from what they have learned from another person; women and slaves (whether male or female) are not admitted as witnesses. However, when a husband's whereabouts are unknown, all the testimonial requirements are disregarded. Testimony that he is dead is accepted even "from one witness, though his testimony is based on what he heard from another man; or even from one woman who learned about it from another woman, or from another slave (male or female)." The final discussion in the Talmud concludes with the words: "In order to prevent the woman from becoming an *agunah*, the rabbis were lenient,"[28] i.e., they did not insist on the strictness of the law. Most illuminating and original is the explanation of Maimonides as to how the rabbis could depart from the generally binding laws of the Torah on this matter:

> The Torah insisted on two witnesses and on the other requirements of the acceptable testimony only in cases where one is completely dependent on the mouth of the witnesses and on their testifying from their own knowledge. For instance, where they testify that one murdered the other, or lent some money to the other. But in matters in which the clarification of the truth does not depend completely on the verbal testimony of this witness, and, in addition, the witness would be unable to excuse himself when in the end it can be proved that his testimony was untrue – for instance, one testifies that someone is dead (i.e., and the person reappears) – the Torah did not insist that the testimony meet all the strict requirements. It would be rather far-fetched to suspect that the witness testified falsely. Therefore, the rabbis were lenient in this matter and believed even one witness testifying on what he has heard from the mouth

28. Yevamot 99a.

of a slave, a woman, etc., so that the daughters of Israel should not become *agunot*.[29]

Even more far-reaching are the innovations designed to limit the husband's power in matters of divorce so as to protect the wife in a situation where, in all fairness, she should not be forced to remain married to him. As is well known, a husband cannot be compelled to grant his wife a divorce; it must be given of his free will. Yet the Mishnah rules that there are certain cases "when we compel him [i.e., to give the *get* and divorce his wife] until he says: 'Yes, I am willing!'"[30] The examples given are: if the husband suffers from *shekhin* (severe boils and inflammation of the skin) or from a sickness of the nose (or the mouth, according to another opinion) that emits a bad odor, or if he follows a profession (e.g., tanning) that causes his body to smell intolerably. In such cases, the wife may say that she cannot endure her husband's condition and is unable to live with him. It is not our intention to enter into a discussion of the difference of opinion between Rabbi Meir and the sages about the specific cases to which this law applies. It is important to realize that at times a wife could indeed not be expected to continue to live with her husband. The rabbis' solution was to compel the husband until he declared that he was willing to divorce his wife freely. Of course, this requires an explanation: how can an enforced act be freely undertaken? Maimonides offers a most original philosophical-psychological explanation,[31] though other interpretations are also possible. It is important to understand that the rabbis faced a serious moral problem – and they had the courage to find a solution. The reason seems to be that the laws of *kiddushin* do not represent the entire Torah. Apart from the right of the husband over divorce, there is another commandment, even more comprehensive and compelling: "And thou shalt love thy neighbor as thyself." It could not be disregarded. There was a conflict between two laws of the Torah. A solution had to be found, and it was found. Its promulgation required a great deal of

29. Maimonides, Gerushin 13, end.
30. Ketubot 77a.
31. Gerushin 2:20.

courage and a deep sense of rabbinical responsibility.

Even more surprising was the treatment of the *moredet* (rebellious woman), i.e., a woman who declares that she is unable to continue married life with her husband. Maimonides formulates the case in this manner: "A woman who refuses to have intercourse with her husband is called *moredet* [rebellious]. One asks her for her reason. If she says, 'I dislike him and am unable to have sexual relations with him freely,' one compels the husband to divorce her. She is not like a prisoner to live with one whom she detests."[32] This is the case closest to the modern concept of incompatibility. Many of the classical authorities, like Rashi and the Rashbam agree with Maimonides' interpretation of the relevant passage in the Talmud; others especially the Rashba, violently disagree with him. According to the Rashba, and those who follow his line of reasoning, such a law would make it possible for the woman to form a liaison with another man and then demand that her husband be compelled to divorce her. This objection is met by Tosafot's comment that the wife's assertion that she cannot continue to live with her husband is accepted "only in cases when her statement is found to have basis in the actual present situation."[33] Important too is the opinion of the Rif to the effect that even though it is not the Talmudic rule to compel the husband to divorce his wife, in such cases "nowadays this is how we decide this matter in the *metivta* [Talmudic academy]: If the woman appears and says, 'I do not want this husband; arrange a *get* for me,' he should give her a *get* immediately."[34] This was indeed the practice for nearly five hundred years in the Babylonian *yeshivot*. Most noteworthy is the decision of the Tashbaz that "if, as we saw, according to the Mishnah the husband is obligated to divorce his wife when, because of his body odor, she cannot be expected to live with him, the same law should be applied to any other case where the wife understandably cannot endure marriage with him." His final conclusion is "that in matters of *shalom bayit* [household peace], everything depends on proper understanding of the situation, and therefore in situations of this kind the rule prevails

32. Ishut 14:8.
33. Ketubot 63b, s.v. *aval amra*.
34. Ibid.

that the *dayan* (rabbinical judge) has to decide in accordance with what his own eyes see."[35]

Most surprising is the Talmudic decision to protect the vital interests of the wife, when need be, by dissolving the marriage retroactively, without any divorce document. The woman is then treated as if she had never been married before. The subject originates in a mishnah. Let us assume that the husband authorized a *shaliah* (representative) to act for him by delivering a *get* into the hands of his wife. Afterwards he goes to a Beth Din and declares that he withdraws the authorization he gave to his *shaliah* and nullifies the get. But he is unable to communicate his withdrawal to the *shaliah*, who goes ahead and delivers the *get* to the wife, as he was asked to do. The wife, of course, now believes that she is divorced and free to remarry. If she does so, however, the consequences might be catastrophic, since in fact she is not divorced but is still legally married to her first husband. The second marriage is invalid and must be terminated. The children, if any, are *mamzerim* (bastards) and are excluded from the community. According to the law, she cannot ever return to her legal husband. In order to avoid such a possibility, Rabban Gamliel the Elder, head of the rabbinical court, instituted the law that a husband was not permitted to invalidate a *get* delivered by a *shaliah* without informing the *shaliah* and the wife, "for the sake of improving the world." However, what happens when a husband disobeys this *takkanah*, and does withdraw the authorization and invalidates the *get*? Rabbi Judah ha-Nasi maintains that the nullification of the *get* by the husband is valid (in spite of all the possible consequences). But Rabban Simeon ben Gamliel says: "The husband's withdrawal is not valid. The *get* retains its legal power. The wife does become divorced." Otherwise, "what would be the value of the authority of the rabbinical court?" The Talmud asks the obvious question: "According to biblical law, the husband has the power to invalidate a *get*, even without the knowledge of his wife, before it reaches his wife. In other words, according to the Torah this woman is still married to her husband. The sages assert the validity of the *get* and declare her to be divorced against

35. Response, sec. 8. A detailed discussion of the entire subject will be found in my *Ha-Halakhah Kohah ve-Tafkidah*, 2nd ed., 5768, pp. 182–193.

the biblical ruling, only because the authority of the rabbinical court would be degraded. How is that possible?" To which a most original and courageous reply is given: "Everyone who espouses a wife does so in accordance with the initially determined rules, in accordance with the rabbinically established conditions. Therefore, if a man violates those conditions, the rabbis have the authority, retroactively, to nullify the act of the marriage."[36]

The extent to which the sages in the Talmud were concerned about the wife's vital interests may be understood from the following story: A childless woman (after ten years of marriage) came before Rav Nahman asking for a *get* and the payment provided in the *ketubah* in the event of a divorce. Rav Nahman told her that since she was demanding the divorce, her husband did not have to pay her; she had no valid reason to request a divorce because unlike her husband, she was not commanded by the Torah to "procreate and multiply." The woman replied that she needed "a cane [to lean on] in her old age and a spade for her burial."[37] In other words, she needed children to support and provide for her in old age and to take care of her burial. The rabbi decided that in such a case "we certainly compel the husband" to meet his wife's demand. Certainly, by Rav Nahman's time the rather primitive status which the Torah had tolerated – the view that that woman was primarily a male-servicing sex object – had been radically changed. The human dignity of women had been greatly established by means of the halakhic institutions and innovations discussed above.

Inheritance

Clearly, the laws of inheritance could not be maintained in their original form. Originally, the biblical rules were promulgated in response to the complaint of the daughters of Zelophehad (see above). They were told that their complaint was justified, but were commanded

36. Gittin 33a; also, e.g., Yevamot 90b and Gittin 73a. An extensive discussion of this subject will be found in my *Tenai be-Nissu'in u-ve-Get.*

37. Yevamot 65b.

to marry men of their own tribe "so that the estates given to the tribes may not be transferred from one tribe to another. As for the children of Israel – everyone should hold on to the estate of his father."[38] This ruling was based on social and economic considerations. Nevertheless, it had to be changed, according to the Talmud, after the generation of Zelophehad's daughters. The rabbis based their rule on a midrashic interpretation of the two words with which the biblical command is introduced: *ve-zeh ha-davar*, "this is the matter." This phrase was taken as meaning, "this is the matter only for the present generation," meaning that the tribes were permitted to intermarry in subsequent generations. The day on which this new ruling was established was the fifteenth of the month of Av, of which Rabban Simeon ben Gamliel said, "There were no holidays in Israel that were celebrated like the fifteen of Av and the Day of Atonement."[39] Unquestionably, such a reinterpretation of the words *zeh ha-davar* is extremely weak. We assume that the rule arose from the experience of the people. In actual practice, it became impossible to maintain the marital separation between the twelve tribes. Gradually, all the other laws of inheritance were adjusted either to practical requirements or in keeping with the restored female dignity in the society.

Another *takkanah* (regulation) departing from the original law of inheritance was introduced because conditions made it necessary. According to biblical law, a husband inherits the dowry of his wife, and when the father of a family dies, his sons inherit his property, which is shared out among all of them. In a polygamous society, this meant that part of the dowry of one wife ultimately passed over into the hands of the sons of another wife. Therefore, fathers were not inclined to provide an adequate dowry for their daughters, who remained unmarried as a result. In order to prevent this, the rabbis introduced a revised marriage contract, known as *ketubat benin dikhrin*, providing that if the wife died, her dowry would be given only to her own sons, and the rest of the father's property was to be divided among all his sons. In essence, this reform was a departure from Torah law, even though the rabbis

38. Numbers 36:6–7.
39. Ta'anit 26b.

of the Talmud found a biblical reason for it in the Torah's rule that a father should make an effort to marry off his daughter.[40] What is truly significant here is that time-conditioned circumstances made it necessary to introduce an innovation that in fact was a change in the biblical law of inheritance.

Another rule of inheritance caused a great deal of discomfort: the law that the husband inherits his wife but she does not inherit from him. The first limitation of the law was introduced with the decision that if a wife's father insists prior to the marriage that the husband shall not inherit his daughter's dowry and whatever else he bestows upon her, his condition is valid and the husband does not inherit his wife's property. Similarly, if the wife's father gave her some property after the marriage, on the condition that her husband have no share in it and not inherit it, his condition is respected.[41]

Another problem arose in a case where the wife died shortly after the marriage. Why should the husband inherit her property? After all, her father gave it to her for her use. If this occurred within a year of the marriage, Rabbenu Tam ruled, the dowry should be returned to her father. Toward the end of his life, however, it appears that Rabbenu Tam changed his mind in this matter. Nevertheless, the *haga'hah* (note) attached to the Rosh quotes:

> I have found written by Rabbenu Tam that he placed a *herem* [ban] on the Jews of France and Lombardy, and they agreed with him, that if the wife dies within a year of her marriage, whatever is left of her dowry and her jewelry should be returned to those who gave them to her or to her heirs. Other communities introduced the rule that if one of the couple should die within two years of their marriage without leaving any offspring, half of the dowry should be returned to the heirs of the departed.[42]

Even more significant was the *takkanah* of the community of Toledo,

40. Ketubot 52b.
41. Gittin 77a, Nazir 24b.
42. Ketubot 47.

specifying that if the wife died during the lifetime of the husband, "and there are healthy offspring, whether a son or a daughter ... whatever is left of her property, the husband should share it – half and half – with that offspring. When she leaves no surviving descendant, all her remaining property belongs to her husband and to those who have a right to inherit her (by family relationship). The husband should hand over half of what he would normally inherit according to biblical law, to the one who has the first claim on her inheritance."[43] Elsewhere the *Tur* emphasizes that since all sorts of practices exist, everything is to be decided in accordance with the accepted rules in the various communities.[44] Even more explicit is the Rivash: "In matters concerning the husband's right to inherit his wife, every community has its own rules or practices. Everyone who marries without making any conditions does so in agreement with the acknowledged *takkanah* or *minhag* prevailing in that community."[45] The Rivash refers to Maimonides for support.

What these new regulations mean is, in essence, a departure from the original law that *kol mah she-kanah ishah kanah ba-alah*, i.e., whatever a wife acquires is acquired by her husband, and whatever remains of her dowry he inherits. The changes became necessary as an act of fairness and justice consequent upon the personal status that the woman acquired in changed condition and under the influence of Torah teaching.

Summing up the results of our study thus far, we have discovered the developing status of women as it passed through two different levels: the Torah-tolerated one and the Torah-guided and Torah-instructed one. On the first and lowest level, in the early man-built and man-maintained society, woman is not recognized as possessing her own personality. At this stage she is merely an impersonal adjunct to the male. It is the Torah-teaching that recognizes her in her own personal existence and establishes her human dignity in a world in which she has her own vitally important place because of her own life-related nature. Only on the impersonal level can there be a rule permitting the

43. *Tur*, Even ha-Ezer 118, beginning.
44. Ibid., chap. 57.
45. Responsa, no. 64.

husband to say to his sick wife, "Here is your *ketubah*, heal yourself with its monetary value or else I will divorce you," when he sees that her medical bills would cause him great monetary loss.[46] Only when a wife is the property of her husband, acquired because of the services she can perform, can such a regulation be legally justified. On the other hand, on the level of woman's Torah-directed personal status, such a rule would violate fundamental ethical principles of the Torah. Our problem today is that the Torah-directed personal status has not as yet completely overcome some elements that have survived from the earlier period. Nothing shows this more convincingly than the way in which Maimonides combined some essential features of the personal and the impersonal status. We have learned of the rabbinical command to love one's wife as oneself and honor her more than oneself. We also noted the wife's duty to look up to her husband as to a prince and take care of all his needs. This is the formulation of Maimonides:

> And thus have our sages commanded that a man should honor his wife more than himself and love her as himself … And thus have they also commanded the wife that she honor her husband "more than enough," that the fear of him should be upon her, and that all her work should be done in accordance with his instruction; he should be in her eyes like a prince or a king who may act as he desires; she should also remove from before him everything that is hateful to him, etc.[47]

It is difficult to understand why Maimonides did not see the contradiction between these two commands. How can a husband who loves and honors his wife, as indicated, want her to fear him, to look up to him as if he were a prince simply because he happens to be her husband, and to remove from his presence everything that might displease him? The truth is that the two principles are mutually exclusive: either you love your wife as yourself and honor her more than yourself, or you demand that she regards you as her lord and master, and serves you accordingly.

46. Maimonides, Ishut 14:18, as above.
47. Ishut 15:19–20.

III "In the Midst of My People I Dwell"

(II Kings 2:13)

It is our task to eliminate whatever remains from the Torah-tolerated, impersonal phase and to establish woman's status completely on the Torah-taught and prescribed personal level. It is obvious that the Talmudic opinions regarding the inadequate intelligence of women no longer have any validity. The view that a woman's knowledge extends only to the spindle might have applied in a society which provided women with only a limited education, but it does not hold today.[1] It is true that the statement was supported by a verse in the Bible. When the Tabernacle was being built in the wilderness, "every woman, wise at heart, was weaving with her hands, etc."[2] Indeed, that was the only significant contribution to the building of the Tabernacle that women were able to make at the time. But certainly the Bible did not state that women in all generations to come would remain incapable of acquiring other knowledge and other abilities. The rabbinic view was a completely time-conditioned, midrashic interpretation. It tells us what Rabbi Eliezer thought about women, but we know now, from actual experience, that the intelligence of women is not below that of their male counterparts. In fact, today's women study and learn and acquire expertise in all of the intellectual and academic disciplines. Rabbi Eliezer's statement[3] that one should not teach Torah to one's daughter because she will craftily misuse her knowledge has lost all its meaning. With the comprehensive education they receive, present-day girls and women are in no need of

1. Yoma 66b.
2. Exodus 35:25.
3. See above; also Sotah 21b; e.g., Rashi's explanation.

Torah study in order to act cunningly, if they so desire. On the contrary, it is just because of their general education that they should study Torah comprehensively and in depth, so that they may integrate their secular knowledge into a Torah-taught worldview of meanings and values.

It may be helpful at this juncture to take a closer look at Rabbi Eliezer's view of women. The story is told that a wise woman asked Rabbi Eliezer the following question: "Why were different punishments meted out for one and the same sin, that of the golden calf?" Rabbi Eliezer did not answer the question, and put her off with the words quoted earlier: "A woman can have no other understanding, except to work at weaving." This, however, is only the first part of the story. In the Jerusalem Talmud, Hyrcanus, Rabbi Eliezer's son, asked his father why he had refused to answer the woman's question. Upon which we hear the surprising answer: "May the words of the Torah be burned rather than be handed over to women."[4] Words like these show that women, for Rabbi Eliezer, were utterly unreliable. How widespread this opinion was may be judged from the fact that the majority of the Talmudic sages disagree with Rabbi Eliezer. And yet, contrary to the generally accepted principle that Halakhah is to be decided according to the majority opinion, in this case, the opinion of the majority was disregarded, and Rabbi Eliezer's view prevailed practically until our own days. As we have indicated, the time has come to disregard completely the minority teaching.

In essence, the issue is inseparable from the idea of trust. As we have shown above, woman was not trusted on the impersonal level in matters of property or in sexual behavior. Obviously, the law that whatever a wife acquires is *eo ipso* acquired by her husband, because otherwise she might steal from him and claim that she has found it, has become not only meaningless but offensively unethical. The twofold lack of trust was justified on the impersonal level. One may trust only a person, a human being, whom one respects or loves. As we learned, the rule was that "a husband should not allow his wife to leave the house more than once in a month, or – if necessary – on a few more occasions," the reason being that "the beauty of a woman lies in her sitting in a corner of her

4. Sotah 3:4.

house, for so it is written, 'the honor of a king's daughter is within.'"[5] I doubt whether there is a single religious family today in which the "king's daughter" conducts herself accordingly. In our time, such a rule would turn the home into a prison for the wife. Women today have the opportunity to "grow up," to develop their potential; they possess a measure of self-respect; they have a place and function in public life. In a mixed society in which the female personality is respected, not every contact between man and woman has sexual significance. When the Talmud says that "women are a people by themselves,"[6] it gives expression to their separation from the life and work of society. It is a radical summing up of the impersonal condition of women as servile adjuncts to the male world. They are excluded because they are seen essentially in their femininity. In this condition, every contact with them is seductive.

The point is clearly illustrated by the well-known saying of Samuel, who declared: *kol be-ishah ervah*, "the voice of a woman is promiscuity."[7] The way this is formulated is worthy of attention. It does not say that a woman's voice is unchaste. That would mean that one must not speak to a woman at all. Therefore, Samuel's law is rendered as follows in the *Shulhan Arukh*: "One should take care not to hear the singing voice of a woman at the recitation of the *Shema Israel* [Hear, O Israel] prayer."[8] Obviously, the idea is that because of the sexual quality of her voice, one would be unable to concentrate on the *Shema*. The Rema rightly adds the comment: "However, her regular voice is not indecent." (The term *ervah* applies only to a married woman. Accordingly, one would be forbidden to listen to the singing of a married woman, but not to that of an unmarried one. However, regarding the *Shema*, one should not listen to the singing of any woman.) It is noteworthy that the phrase *kol be-ishah* ("the voice in a woman") is parallel to the saying of Rav Hisda: *shok be-ishah ervah*, "the naked thigh of a woman is *ervah*."[9]

5. Maimonides, Ishut 14:11.
6. Shabbat 62b.
7. Berakhot 24a.
8. Chap. 75, par. 35.
9. Berakhot 24a.

In other words, to listen to the singing of a woman is as indecent as to view her naked thigh. One cannot help wondering how sexual implications of the two acts could ever have been considered equal. At the same time, one cannot overlook the fact that the words in the Song of Songs (*Shir ha-Shirim*) upon which Samuel bases his statement have, indeed, a sensual meaning. The lover says to his beloved: "Let me see thy countenance, let me hear thy voice; for sweet is thy voice, and thy countenance is comely."[10] And in the same context: "My beloved is mine, and I am his." This, of course, is not an everyday occurrence. It is hardly believable that Samuel should have turned the words "for sweet is your voice" out of their specific meaning, spoken in a highly amorous situation, and attributed their quality to the voice of every woman all the time and in every situation.

There is only one explanation: on the impersonal level of exclusion from society, woman's character appears foremost in her sensuality. Thus, every contact with her has an element of sexual seduction. All this no longer has any validity in an age when, on the basis of Torah ideals, woman has been acknowledged in her personal humanity, and has been integrated into the comprehensive structure of human existence. Nowadays, the singing of a woman is not fundamentally different from what the original Halakhah termed "her regular voice." A woman's voice, even when she is singing, is nothing unusual today, and it is no more distracting during the *Shema* prayer than that of a man singing. Only in specific amorous situations, as in the Song of Songs, may it have a sensual quality.

In the same way, a number of other statements about women no longer apply. As we saw, one of the most negative sayings about women is found in the Midrash: "Women are not capable of teaching, nor may one rely on their words."[11] A statement like this should be disregarded. It might have been justified in its time, but today the words of women are no less reliable than those of men. Nor is there any reason to claim that women who have the right kind of education and learning are incapable of teaching. Similarly, it may once have been justified for

10. Song of Songs 2:44.
11. Midrash Numbers Rabbah 10.

the Talmud to say that women should not teach children, because this would bring them into contact with their fathers,[12] but we have now reached a stage in which the numerous daily contacts between men and women are free of seductive qualities, and as a result this rule, too, has lost its meaning. In light of all this, there is little doubt that woman's status, both in marriage and in society, has to be revised. There is ample precedent for doing so.

Let us consider some further halakhic consequences of the new situation. As we have already seen, the husband's power over his wife was curbed and limited in several areas. A husband might be required to divorce his wife "by his own free will" when the wife could not be expected to continue to remain with him. In such cases, the *Beth Din* would pressure the husband until he was ready to agree to give his wife the desired *get* of his own "free will." This solution was applied even when the wife declared that her only reason for desiring a divorce was incompatibility between the two of them. Moreover, there are cases where, because of the husband's disregard of rabbinical rules or violations of generally accepted canons of behavior, the marriage was retroactively annulled.

In our days, the situation in matters of divorce is intolerable. In numerous cases, after a marriage has broken down, the husband exploits his power either to refuse to give his wife a *get* altogether, or to dictate onerous conditions, especially in regard to property or money. This causes a great deal of suffering for many wives. The injustice involved is extremely serious and represents a *hillul Hashem*, a desecration of the divine name. The cases described above should be treated as precedents to follow in our own time. In my *T'nai be-Nissu'in u-ve-Get*, I have shown that there is ample halakhic basis for the inclusion of needed and appropriate conditions in the marriage contract (*ketubah*), even including a provision specifying that if either party to the marriage refuses to fulfill the mutually agreed conditions, the marriage becomes annulled retroactively.

A similar revision is needed regarding the property rights of the wife. In this area, too, there is ample halakhic precedent. Quite clearly, as we

12. Kiddushin 84a.

saw in the preceding chapters, the original biblical law of inheritance, according to which only sons inherit the father, was justified in the era when the land was divided among the tribes of the children of Israel. Had daughters been entitled to inherit, intertribal marriages would have led to the accumulation of large shares of the land by some tribes to the detriment of others. Since the dispersion of the tribes from the land of Israel and the destruction of the state, this law no longer applies. However, another law of inheritance requires a review. As we learned, in case of the wife's death, the husband inherits her property; e.g., her dowry. On the other hand, she does not inherit her husband's estate. As to the first law, we noted that it was gradually eroded and finally disregarded. Already in the Talmud, it was determined that a father could make a premarital condition that the husband would not inherit what he gave his daughter on her marriage. Similarly, even though the rule was that what a woman acquired was acquired by her husband, there was an important exception to this rule. People could give her gifts or any kind of property with the condition that her husband have no share in it. Later on, after the conclusion of the Talmud, we found that in various communities all kinds of *takkanot* (regulations) were introduced which limited the validity of the husband's right to his wife's property. Of course, all this was done prior to the marriage, so that the husband was familiar with the terms and accepted them. Even after the marriage there was a way of disregarding the husband's claim to her inheritance. Nachmanides decided that the wife could make a condition that after her husband inherited her he would turn the inheritance over to her heirs. Finally we reach the summation: "However in every community there are *takkanot* and *minhagim*, 'regulations and customs,' in these matters; generally, anyone who marries does so in accordance with the customs and practices among them, as already Maimonides determined it."[13] All of this was in keeping with the rule that before the marriage it was possible to make the condition that would eliminate the husband's right to inherit his wife.

As for the other aspect of the law of inheritance, determining that the wife does not inherit her husband's property, it is undoubtedly a survival

13. Rivash, Responsa, no. 64.

from the era of woman's impersonal, subservient status. Accordingly, the sons inherit the father's property and are to support their widowed mother from it. Can such a law be maintained with good conscience in a society in which the husband is taught to love his wife as himself and honor her more than himself? How can it be reconciled with the warning that Rabbi Judah ha-Nasi gave his sons on his deathbed, to "take extreme care regarding the honor of your mother," or the words of Rabbi Joseph who, when he heard his mother's footsteps, said, "I shall stand before the divine presence that has arrived." Quite clearly, different legal arrangements are needed for determining property rights in marriage as well as in matters of inheritance in the case of the death of the wife or the husband. All this is possible in accordance with the Halakhah; for in monetary matters conditions agreed upon by the parties concerned are legally valid. Normally, one would say that in this area the law of the country should prevail, in accord with the principle of *dina demalkhuta dina*, i.e., the law of the country is halakhically acknowledged law. But, of course, it is conceivable that both parties will agree to specific conditions in certain individual cases.

Certain halakhic rules regarding the function of women in public life also require revision. According to Halakhah, a woman is not admitted as a witness. We saw, at least in one case, that an exception was made in order to protect a wife against becoming an *agunah*. We also noted Maimonides' explanation that all the exceptions in this case (i.e., one witness, etc.; see above) could be made because the purpose of the law about witnesses was to establish the truth. In the case in which the exceptions were allowed, it was reasonable to assume that an otherwise not accepted testimony was reliable. We must ask ourselves whether it is reasonable to believe that today a woman's testimony would be less reliable than a man's. We have determined that the statement that the words of women are not reliable no longer has any truth value. Today's women have a comprehensive education, including thorough Torah study, are active professionally, and are acknowledged in their own personalities: they are clearly no less trustworthy than men.

It is true that the exclusion of women from appearing as witnesses is based on a verse in the Torah.[14] However, there is a very important precedent for the acceptance of a woman as a judge – Deborah. Tosafot asks how Deborah could be a judge, since someone who is disqualified as a witness cannot be a judge.[15] The answer given is: "Most likely she could function as a judge because the people accepted her on account of the Shekhinah [divine presence] that was with her." It is important to understand that it was not the presence of the Shekhinah that qualified her. The Shekhinah was the reason why the people accepted her and submitted to her authority. Her acceptance by the people was decisive. It was the people from whom she derived her authority.

Such is, indeed, the Halakhah. People have the right to appoint someone as a judge over them or to trust him as a witness, even though normally he would not be qualified for those tasks. A person has the right to submit himself to an unqualified judge or witness. A father cannot judge for a son, neither in his favor nor against him. Yet in a case that requires legal judgment, if one party is willing to accept his own father or the other party's father as a judge, then either father, as the case may be, has the authority to function for the two parties as a judge whose decision is binding. In fact, in many communities in which courts were established to rule in matters of communal concern, it was also customary, as a rule, to allow even relatives to testify in matters of communal interest.[16] Not to admit women as witnesses on the basis of their acceptance by the community of the Jewish people would be to exclude them from the male world. However, as we determined above, the principle of exclusion has lost its validity in the phase of women's Torah-taught personal status. Indeed, in view of women's share in social life and their role in it, the exclusively male world does not exist any longer.

The same holds for the question of appointing women to public office. The Torah says: "Thou shalt appoint a king over you."[17] The Sifrei comments: "A king but not a queen." This rule became the law.

14. Shevuot 30a.
15. Bava Kama 15a.
16. See, e.g., Rashba, Responsa, 680.
17. Deuteronomy 17:14.

A woman could not rule as queen. Maimonides adds: "Thus, all appointments in Israel are to be male."[18] Maimonides combines the appointment of kings with other offices of authority, even though the Bible only mentions the office of the king. Obviously, he felt that both have the same reason. According to the *Kesef Mishneh*,[19] the source for this rule was the mishnah in *Kiddushin* which states that all dealings with women (in all kinds of work activities) lead to evil practices.[20]

Once again we are up against "women being a people by themselves," which has been completely overturned now that woman's Torah-prescribed personal existence has ended her seclusion in a corner of her home as befits a princess. What is more, public offices today are fundamentally different from what they were in the age of the Israelite monarchy. The king was appointed by the Sanhedrin and a prophet. He was an absolute monarch, not accountable to the people. And all appointments derived their authority from the monarchic order. It is important to pay careful attention to the exact biblical text in this matter. It reads: "Appoint a king over you"; the king was appointed to be above the people. And similarly all the lower dignitaries in this monarchial system were appointed to rule above the people. Today, there are rules and regulations for all public offices, whose authority derives from the will of the people. Public officials function on the basis of their acceptance by the people. As we saw, such acceptance has validity with the support of the halakhic system of Judaism. There is a surprising precedent for a woman being active in public affairs. The prophet Elisha wished to express his gratitude to the Shunnamite for the generous hospitality she had extended to him. In her presence, he had his young servant say to her: "Behold, you have so anxiously taken care of us. What can we do for you? Is there anything you would have us talk to the king about, or to the head of the army?" Her answer was: "I dwell in the midst of my people," which the Targum Yonatan renders: "I am engaged in the affairs of my people [i.e., and carry the burden of

18. Melakhim 1:4.
19. Ibid.
20. Kiddushin 82b.

the community]."[21] This indeed should be the essence of women's status in Judaism: I live in the midst of my people, and take my share in caring for the communal needs in accordance with my ability.

21. See Pahad Yitzhak, s.v. *zibbur*.

IV Contemporary Halakhic Issues Regarding Women

In this chapter, I intend to present in a concise manner some conclusions that I reached in a halakhic study based, in a comprehensive manner, on the relevant Talmudic sources and the classical commentators and codifiers.

1. SELF-OBLIGATION BY WOMEN

By "self-obligation" I refer to the practice whereby women impose upon themselves the responsibility of fulfilling certain commandments which biblical law does not require them to fulfill, i.e., *mitzvoth aseh she-ha-zeman geramah* (time-dependent *mitzvot*). This subject would seem to be of little interest today, since it has become customary for women to fulfill such *mitzvot*. For example, the blowing of the shofar on Rosh Hashanah and the commandment of the *lulav* and *etrog* (together with the other two plants) on the festival of Sukkot are widely practiced by women. It may then be taken for granted that women *do* have the right to accept for themselves the practice of *mitzvot* from which the Torah freed them. All the relevant questions are discussed in the Babylonian as well as the Jerusalem Talmud and the recognized commentaries and codes.

Once the decision of the Babylonian Talmud[1] was followed in the matter of self-imposed *mitzvot*, there were some important questions that had to be clarified: are women permitted to say the *berakhah* (blessing)

1. Arakhin 96a.

before performing the mitzvah? Since they are not obligated by Torah law, isn't their *berakhah* unnecessary and their pronunciation of God's name in vain? Secondly, how can they say the prescribed word *tzivanu*, "and commanded us," when in fact they have not been commanded? And finally, according to the biblical law one may not add to the *mitzvot* of the Torah, but if women voluntarily practice *mitzvot*, are they not introducing an addition to the Torah?

The last question did not trouble the commentators very much, for it could easily be resolved. One is adding to the *mitzvot* of the Torah only if the added practice is genuinely new. If one were to add a fifth plant to the four festival plants of *lulav*, that would be a transgression of the law of *lo tosifu*, "thou shalt not add not take away anything" from the commandments of the Torah. But to practice a mitzvah of the Torah even though one is not ordered to is not to change the form of the realization of the mitzvah by adding anything new and alien to the Torah. Rabbi Joseph Karo, in his commentary on the Tur, rejects the idea that women performing *mitzvot* not commanded them could be a question of adding to the Torah, saying: "That is not right at all."[2] Unfortunately, he does not give his reasons. Instead he concludes his comment with the words: "However, I do not have to elaborate on this."

As for the question of the validity of the phrase *tzivanu*, there is, for instance, the answer of the Ran (Rabbenu Nissim), based on the generally acknowledged principle that "the one who is commanded and does is greater than the one who is not commanded and yet does." The reference to "one who is not commanded and yet does" indicates that although this practice does not have the same value as doing because one is commanded, yet it also has a value. Similarly, the *berakhah* on the lighting of the Hanukah candles includes the term *ve-tzivanu*, even though nowhere in the Torah are we commanded to perform that mitzvah. The Ran concludes his explanation: "Since men were commanded even *mitzvot* from which they were originally free and women's action is also appreciated, women too may well say: 'And has commanded us.'"

There remains the first problem that we indicated: since women

2. Orah Hayyim 589.

are not commanded about the time-bound *mitzvot* (*mitzvot aseh she-ha-zeman geramah*), are they not pronouncing the Name of God in vain when they say a blessing that is not required? Here we reach a disagreement between the giants of halakhic teaching. According to Rabbenu Tam, the Name of God pronounced in a *berakhah* is not in vain and therefore it may be used.[3] Accordingly, women who obligate themselves may say the accepted formula of the blessing and do the mitzvah. However, Rashi and the Rambam (Maimonides) disagree with this opinion and rule that while women may practice the *mitzvot* in question, they are not permitted to say the *berakhah* over them. This disagreement between the halakhic authorities need not trouble us either. The majority of the halakhic teachers accept the opinion of Rabbenu Tam. Here is the final decision as given by the Rema in the *Shulhan Arukh*: "The custom is that women do say the *berakhah* over the time-related commandments [i.e., *mitzvot aseh she-ha-zeman geramah*]."[4]

After all that clarification, we are confronted with an utterly unexpected surprise. The Rema, having stated that women do say the *berakhah* over *mitzvot aseh she-ha-zeman geramah*, in the section of the *Shulhan Arukh* on the laws of *tefillin*, writes: "If women wish to impose [the putting on of *tefillin*] upon themselves, one does not permit it."[5] What are the reasons and the source for this statement? It seems to contradict everything that is said on the subject in the Talmud. According to the Babylonian Talmud, women are not obligated to put on the phylacteries, but if they wish to, they may do so. According to the Jerusalem Talmud, the sages did not allow the daughter of King Saul to put on *tefillin*, the reason being that since she was not obligated, she must not perform the mitzvah on her own. In the Jerusalem Talmud, as in the Babylonian Talmud, the commandment of *tefillin* is the example for all other *mitzvot* whose fulfillment depends on the sequence of time, but in the Babylonian Talmud, women may take on a self-imposed obligation, whereas in the Jerusalemite one, they are not allowed to do so.

3. Berakhot 21a.
4. Orah Hayyim 589: 6, 17:2.
5. Ibid. 38:3.

According to both teachings, however, since *tefillin* is time-bound (e.g., no *tefillin* on Shabbat), whatever applies to *tefillin* in the case of women is the law for all other commandments that are, like *tefillin*, dependent on time-sequence. One cannot help wondering how the commandment of the *tefillin* can be an exception. Since *tefillin* is the prototype for all time-bound commandments, and whatever applies to it applies to all, how can it be maintained that woman are free from *mitzvot aseh she-ha-zeman geramah* yet may obligate themselves, but not regarding the mitzvah of *tefillin*? Actually, nowhere in the Talmud itself is there any basis for such an exception. The opinion of the Rema is based on a passage in the Mekhilta maintaining that Michal, the daughter of King Saul, was not allowed to put on *tefillin*. Tosafot now explains the reason of the Pesikta: *tefillin* requires a "clean body" and women are not careful with bodily hygiene. The Pesikta would be equal in authority to the Talmud. But we have to realize that the reason for the Pesikta's decision is not found in its text. The explanation was added by the Tosafot, and was accepted by some, until finally it was included in the *Shulhan Arukh* by the Rema.

Obviously, the lack of bodily cleanliness attributed to women cannot be in reference to the monthly period. If so, women would indeed be an exception, but the reason would have nothing to do with *mitzvot* determined by time. The whole structure of separating such commandments into a group by themselves would not be justified. How then is the opinion regarding the lack of bodily hygiene to be understood? The Magen Avraham, in his commentary, apparently seeks to resolve this problem, though he does not make explicit mention of it.[6] Explaining the words of the Rema, he quotes the statement of the Tosafot that we have quoted above. However, he adds: "But if women were obligated by biblical law to fulfill the *tefillin* commandment, they would be more careful about their bodily cleanliness." The Magen Avraham wishes to say that the original Talmudic conclusion that women are free from the commandment of donning *tefillin* has nothing to do with the question of how well they care for their bodies. For if they were commanded to do the mitzvah, they would be competent in

6. Ibid.

matters of hygiene demanded by the mitzvah of the phylacteries.

Thus, the only reason for freeing women from this commandment could be the quality of the dependence of the obligation of fulfillment on the sequence of time. If so, we conclude that commandments in this category are not obligatory on women. In Talmudic sources the question of bodily hygiene does not enter into consideration. On the contrary, according to the Babylonian Talmud, which has been accepted as the valid law, the daughter of King Saul did practice the mitzvah of *tefillin*, and so too may all women. The opinion that nevertheless women should not be allowed to put on *tefillin* because of their hygienic carelessness with their bodies is a later post-Talmudic development. The authors who accepted this idea obviously were doing so on the basis of their own experience: such were the women they knew, the women of their time. Let us state unequivocally that nowadays such an evaluation of female behavior would be utterly unjustified and a serious insult to womankind. In matters of bodily hygiene, women are at least as reliable as men. We may completely disregard the opinion of the Rema in this matter and follow such authorities as Rashi, Rabbenu Tam, Rambam, and Rashba, who make no distinction between the commandment of *tefillin* and the other *mitzvot aseh she-ha-zeman geramah*. The *Hagahot Maimoniyot* (i.e., the commentary on the work of Maimonides) quotes the *Sar M'kuzi* that women may make the *berakhah* on *lulav* and *tefillin* and all similar *mitzvot*.[7] Women today may well be guided by these authorities.

2. WOMEN'S PRAYER SERVICES

The effort by some Orthodox women to have their own prayer services has aroused serious discussion and even disagreement. One might wonder why this matter should have become such a heated issue. The status of women has fundamentally changed in comparison to previous generations. Their general education is not below that of men. They take an active part in the affairs of the community, in the educational

7. On Maimonides, Hilkhot Tzizit 3:40, end.

system, in synagogue activities, in maintaining organizations whose work is essential for the life of the Jewish people. If women of today, out of their desire to have a more active share in the religious practices of Judaism, wish to organize prayer services for themselves similar to the *tefillah be-tzibbur* (communal services) of men, why should that not be welcomed!? Women have the same obligation to pray as men. While only men, and not women, are commanded to study the Torah and therefore are obligated to read the Torah, this does not mean that women are not permitted to read it. The Talmud states clearly that women may be included among the seven people called to the Torah (on Shabbat), although it adds: "Yet women should not read the Torah during services because of the dignity of the community." Be this as it may, obviously it has no significance for women reading the Torah in a prayer assembly of women. As for the saying of the *berakhah* before and after the reading, as is customary in synagogues, the question has been discussed by the halakhic authorities, for instance Tosafot and others. Their ruling may be summed up unequivocally that women no less than men may recite the well-known blessings over the Torah. One of the arguments advanced in support of this ruling is that the Torah blessings do not include the words *asher kideshanu be-mitzvotav ve-tzivanu*, "who has sanctified us by His commandments and commanded us." And women, indeed, were not commanded to study the Torah. Much more simply, it is added that the blessing over the Torah is included in the daily prayers that women recite every day. Rather significant is the further explanation of the Bakh, who says: "Since women are obligated to study the *mitzvot* which are addressed to them, therefore they may well say the *berakhah* over the Torah every day, etc."[8]

Since women are obligated to pray and may also read the Torah, why should they not be permitted to have their own public prayer service, if that grants them deeper religious satisfaction, and a more meaningful sense of having the commandment of prayer than by being present in the synagogue during the community services, in which they have no share at all?

8. Tosafot on Eruvin 96a, Rosh ha-Shanah 33a; Bah on *Tur*, Yoreh De'ah 246; also Orah Hayyim 47.

Of course, one might perhaps argue that communal prayer (*tefillah be-tzibbur*) is much more important and is much more a fulfillment of the mitzvah to pray than is prayer in a woman's service. The women's service, no matter how many participate in it, remains *tefillat yahid*, the private prayer of individuals. Thus the Torah reading at a women's service is not the fulfillment of the mitzvah in its completeness, as is that in a synagogue. Indeed, why not say that women should remain with their prayers in the synagogue, just as they fulfill other commandments that they are not obligated to practice – commandments like *shofar* and *lulav* – in the manner they are done by men? The difference is obvious. When women do the *mitzvot* that are *ha-zeman geramah*, dependent on the time-sequence, they are in fact fulfilling a commandment. However, by their presence at the communal service they do not reach the category of *eino metzuveh ve-aseh*, i.e., those who are not commanded and yet they do. Their prayers in a synagogue do not change in essence and do not become part of the *tefillat tzibbur*. Indeed, women are outside the community, and even in the synagogue their prayer remains *tefillat yahid*, the prayer of an individual. There is indeed a great deal of difference between communal and individual prayer, but only for men. Only for them is *tefillah be-tzibbur* of greater importance than *tefillat yahid*. For women, however, *tefillah be-tzibbur* is an impossibility. For that very reason, their individual prayer is no less significant and meaningful that the communal prayer of men. One can even say that the prayer experience in a women's service may be much more meaningful to the participants than being present at communal services from which they feel completely excluded. Nothing could be more wrong than to assert that by holding their own services women separate themselves from the community. On the contrary, their own services in common bring them nearer to the experience of Jewish unity as intended by the Torah.

A more serious aspect of the issue with which we are dealing is the allegation that women's services represent the introduction of a new *minhag* (custom) into the prayer order of the Jewish people. The question is of a twofold nature. First of all, is this new custom contrary to what has been followed in the Jewish communities? Secondly, do we have the right to establish new *minhagim* (customs) that were unknown in the generations before us? The responsa to the first question is relatively easy, on the basis of the generally accepted halakhic principle that *lo ra'iynu eino rayah*, i.e., not having seen a certain halakhic practice is no proof that what was not done should not be done now either. It is clear that the fact that women in previous generations did not organize "communal" services for themselves is no proof that such services must not be introduced at all. May we say that whatever has not yet been done in matters of the fulfillment of *mitzvot* must never be done?

Yet there does seem to be proof that in the case of *minhagim* (customary behavior) *lo ra'inu*, that a *minhag* was not known, its very nonexistence, *raya*, is proof that nonobservance is the correct custom and must not be changed. We shall discuss here only one example that is in itself revealing for all the other cases of this kind. According to the first mishnah in Tractate Hullin, *ha-kol shohatin*, i.e., all may perform the act of slaughtering animals as required by the law of the Torah. The Talmud explains that the word *ha-kol*, "all," includes women. Women, too, may perform this command. Nonetheless, there is an authority, the *Agur*, who asserts: "I have never seen women do slaughtering of animals; therefore, we do not allow them to do it. The *minhag* annuls the halakhah. The customs of our fathers are Torah."[9] This seems to suggest that in the case of customs, their very nonpractice is proof enough not to change the generally accepted behavior. This would mean that since women's prayer services were not customary in former times, the institution of such services today violates the old established custom of not having such services. The very fact that such services did not exist would be sufficient proof not to introduce them now.

Such an argument would miss completely the essential quality – the halakhic background – of the statement we have quoted above, based on the example of the slaughtering of animals by women. According to the Mishnah, women have the right to do *shehitah* (slaughtering). Nevertheless, the *Hilkhot Eretz Yisrael* taught that women should not do it. Their weaker constitution might cause them to faint in the act. However, Tosafot maintains that this is the personal view of the *Hilkhot Eretz Yisrael* and need not be followed. Tosafot concludes that, as taught in the Mishnah, women may well practice *shehitah*. Most of the other

9. His comment on the Rif, Berakhot 20b.

halakhic authorities agree with this ruling. It is with reference to this decision that the *Agur* says: "Even though that is the opinion of the authorities, the custom in all Israel is that women do not do *shehitah*. I myself have never seen anything to the contrary. Therefore, one should not allow them to perform *shehitah*. For the *minhag* annuls the halakhah. The custom of our fathers is Torah." In this case, there were two rulings: that of Tosafot, "for it" and that of *Hilkhot Eretz Yisrael*, "against it." In this instance the acceptance of the ruling not to allow women to slaughter animals was not just "not-doing," but an "active" rejection of the ruling of Tosafot and the other authorities. It was saying: "No! We are not following your opinion." This, indeed, is the norm. In all the other cases which are quoted to show that *lo ra'iynu* is *ra'aya* (proof), there are always two opinions, one for the practice, the other against it. In all these cases the nonpractice is a rejection of an opposing ruling. Where, however, there is no opposing ruling the nonpractice of an activity does not establish it as a *minhag* that must not be changed. In such cases the principle remains valid that *lo ra'iynu eino rayah*, that the nonpractice is itself no proof that a *minhag* exists that must not be changed. In former times women generally did not go to the synagogue. Shall we therefore say that women should not change the custom and should not go to synagogue services? In the time of the Magen Avraham women did not listen to the reading of the Torah. During the Torah reading, writes the Magen Avraham, women would leave the synagogue.[10] Shall we now argue that because it was not customary for women to attend the Torah reading, it is now not permitted for them to violate the *minhag* and listen to the Torah reading? The same applies to women's services. Their nonexistence was not due to any rejection of an existing demand for such services. The situation was entirely different from what it is today. We never saw such services before because women did not have the kind of education and participation in the life of the community that they have today. No one called for such services because no one felt the need for them. The nonpractice of women's services was not a *minhag*, and to introduce them in our times is not violating an established custom.

With this we have also answered our second question, as to whether

10. Orah Hayyim 282:6.

we are permitted to create new *minhagim* that were not known to previous generations. There is no doubt that new customs that were not known before, and were instituted because of the social and educational changes that have taken place, are not contrary to the *minhagim* of previous generations. It may be helpful to recall Rashi's significant explanation of the well-known Talmudic saying: "*Elu ve-elu divrei Elokim Hayyim*," meaning that when two Talmudic scholars disagree, the teachings of both are the words of the living God, even though the Halakhah is decided only according to one of them. Explains Rashi: "At times one reason applies, at other times the other reason may be valid. Reasons may change as conditions change even to a small extent."[11] If that is the rule even in regard to small changes in conditions, and even in matters of biblical command, how much more is one to be guided by it in matters which have their origin in later rabbinical rules, as, for instance, prayer and prayer services?

One may well illustrate the point with the help of two responsa in the work of my teacher, Gaon Rabbi Yehiel Yaakov Weinberg, of blessed memory. In one of the responsa in the third volume of his *Seridei Esh*, he discusses the question of whether it is permissible, in order to eliminate the pain caused by circumcision, to administer some form of anesthetic to a child, a convert, or any Jew who was not circumcised as a child. In another responsa he discusses the question of the Bat Mitzvah celebration for girls when they reach the age that obligates them to keep the *mitzvot*, as one celebrates the Bar Mitzvah of boys at the age of thirteen.

In both responsa the problem is the same; i.e., is one permitted to introduce new *minhagim* that were not practiced before? In the first question he reaches the conclusion that no anesthetics may be given to eliminate the pain of circumcision. He argues that the possibility of administering a drug to enable a person to endure the circumcision painlessly existed even in Talmudic times. Yet it was not done. The problem then was not different from what it is today. Therefore, it should not be done today either. He concludes with the words: "*Minhag Yisrael Torah hi*," "The custom of Israel is Torah; one must not offend it."

11. Rashi on Ketubot 57a, s.v. *ha'k'mashma lan.*

As to the second question, he fully supports the introduction of the Bat Mitzvah celebration. He writes: "That it was not done in previous generations is indeed no argument. The generations before us did not have to occupy themselves with the upbringing of daughters as we do today." After further elaborating this point, Rabbi Weinberg concludes: "The rules of honest logic and the pedagogic principle almost compel us to celebrate for our daughters too, their reaching the age that obligates them to observe the commandments of the Torah. The discrimination between sons and daughters as regards their maturity is a serious insult to the sense of human dignity of the growing daughter, etc."

The difference between the two cases is clear. In the first case, there has been no change whatever in the conditions of the times. The problem has always existed. The possibility of eliminating the pain by means of some drug or, later on, some injection, has always been available. Yet the rabbis did not make use of it. This means that they were against it. Their ruling established the *minhag* for further generations as well. *Minhag Yisrael Torah hi* – a *minhag* of this kind is Torah. As for the Bat Mitzvah, the fact that it was not practiced in former times did not establish a *minhag*. There was no such celebration because there was no need for it, nor would there have been any understanding of it. That was no *minhag*, but an unplanned and unintended absence, a complete vacuum. Today, however, conditions have changed. The Bat Mitzvah celebration does not abolish anything; it does not antagonize any *minhag*. It has a meaningful function in the context of Torah observance.

All this also applies to the introduction of women's prayer services in our time. Their absence in the past does not mean that this should remain so for all time to come. It was in conformity with the prevailing conditions. The new practice does not offend what there was, for what there was is no more.

Nor is there any reason why women should not rejoice with the Torah scroll on Simhat Torah, especially now that women study the Torah more than ever before. Apart from the small group of *mitzvot aseh she-ha-zeman geramah* (commandments dependent on the time sequence), they are obligated to observe all the commandments of the Torah (exclusive of Torah study). Why should they not rejoice over the One "who gave us a Torah of Truth and planted eternal life in our midst"? "Us" means the Jewish people, and "in our midst" is in the midst of all Israel.

There remains just one more point that requires elucidation, the principle that "every sacred service requires a minyan," a quorum of ten male participants. First, we must bear in mind that this is not a biblical command. Noting that the reciting of the *Shema* is undoubtedly a *davar she-bi-kedushah* (sacred prayer), Rabbenu Jonah tells us that there is nothing in our prayers more sacred than the words expressing our acceptance of the yoke of God's rule, yet the *Shema* does not require a quorum of ten and may well be recited individually. Therefore, the phrase "every sacred service" cannot be taken literally.

The meaning of the principle can only be that every prayer that was originally instituted as requiring ten people must be so observed. Since the recitation of the *Shema* was never so established, it may be recited in private even though it is holier than the other prayers that have the character of *kedushah* (i.e., holiness). One may, however, ask: if the requirement of the quorum of ten was originally instituted by the rabbis, how are we to understand the Talmudic explanation that the rule is derived from a verse in the Torah, "And I shall be sanctified in the midst of the children of Israel," interpreting "in the midst" as in the midst of a minimum of ten?

Undoubtedly the derivation from the Bible is not to be taken literally. First of all, the various daily services are not a biblical command but a rabbinical *takkanah*_(arrangement). Secondly, the biblical words "And I shall be sanctified in the midst of the children of Israel" require *Kiddush Hashem* (the sanctification of the divine name by sacrificing oneself even if one's life is threatened, rather than deny God in public). Now, this command has nothing to do with prayer services, nor does it discriminate between men and women. In the given situation, all Jews are obligated to *Kiddush Hashem* (sanctification of the divine name). This verse in the Bible, stating that one needs a public quorum of at least ten in order to recite some of the more sacred parts of the prayer service, like the *kedushah* and *Barhu*, is used as what is known as an *asmakhta*, a borrowed biblical verse on which a rabbinical institution "leans" for support. But then, of course, one may ask whence the basis for the determination that only men may form a minyan. The original meaning of the biblical support does not distinguish between male and female children of Israel. The fact is that nowhere in the Talmud where the quorum of ten is mentioned is it stated that the ten must all be men. The exclusion of women from the communal service can only be another rabbinical arrangement added to the first rabbinical *takkanah* of public prayer with ten members. What might have been the reason for this additional requirement, for which the biblical verse cannot be used even as an *asmakhta*, a borrowed support? Quite clearly, it could not have been that women lack the purity needed. As we saw, the *Shema* is a more sacred prayer than any of the parts of the daily prayer for which a minyan of ten males is required, yet it is prayed even in private by men and women alike. The reason for the exclusion of women from the *tefillah be-tzibbur* (communal prayer) can only be that the rabbis would not allow men and women to pray together. If that is so, one might give serious consideration to the halakhic possibility of a female minyan, i.e., of allowing the recitation of *Kedushah* and *Barhu* at women's prayers services in the presence of a minimum of ten women.

3. BIRKAT HA-MAZON

The Mishnah states explicitly that women are obligated to say grace after meals. Since *Birkat ha-Mazon* is not dependent on the time of day, it is not a *mitzvah aseh she-ha-zeman geramah*. This point is so obvious that the Talmud has to explain why it is necessary to state it in a mishnah. Yet the Talmudic explanation includes a discussion of whether women's obligation to say grace is a rabbinical one or is based on the biblical command: "And you shall eat and be satisfied and bless the Eternal One, your God."[12] Upon the difference between the two kinds of commandments depends the right of a woman to fulfill the mitzvah on behalf of others who are present and listen to her recitation.

According to the law, one may fulfill a commandment for the sake of others only if one is under the same obligation as are those for whom one is to act. If the woman's duty to say *Birkat ha-Mazon* is

12. Berakhot 20b.

only rabbinical and she has no such obligation under Torah law, she cannot say grace for a man, since his obligation is biblical. At first, the Talmud attempts to bring a proof that a woman's obligation is biblical (*mi-deoraita*), arguing from a *baraita* stating that a son may say grace for his father, and a woman, for her husband. If the woman's duty were only rabbinical, how could she act validly for her husband? This proof, however, is pushed aside with the argument that the son is probably a minor. But how can a minor son perform a mitzvah on behalf of his father? Presumably he can say grace for his father in this instance only because the father has eaten less than the measure of food that requires the saying of grace according to the Torah. Not having eaten the requisite amount, the father is only under a rabbinical obligation, just like his minor son. From this, it becomes evident that even if a woman's duty is only of rabbinical origin, she may say grace for her husband in an eventuality where his obligation is also only rabbinical.[13]

According to Tosafot and the Rosh, the question of whether a woman's obligation to say grace is biblical or rabbinical has not been finally decided.[14] Maimonides also holds that the question remains in doubt. However, there are also other opinions. The *Tur* quotes the Rabad to the effect that women's duty to say grace after meals is biblical. Relying on the plain meaning of the *baraita* that a woman may say *Birkat ha-Mazon* for her husband, he disregards the possibility that it might apply when the husband did not eat the amount of food that would have obligated him as a biblical command. The Ran agrees with this interpretation.[15]

The main reason for those who maintain that the woman's obligation is biblical is quoted by the *Bet Yosef* in the name of the Rashba. The disagreement in the Talmud is between Ravina, who believes that the woman's obligation is only rabbinical, and Rava, who insists that it is biblical. But Rava was Ravina's teacher, so his authority supersedes that of Ravina. Therefore, we follow Rava's teaching that women have to say grace as a biblical command. There are other halakhic authorities who

13. Ibid.
14. Ibid.
15. Ran on ibid. and on Sukkah 38a; *Tur* and *Bet Yosef*, Orah Hayyim 186.

take the same view, among them, for instance, the *Or Zarua.*[16]

It is surprising that the halakhah in the *Shulhan Arukh* has been decided according to those who maintain that the question is still open and remains in doubt. The law of *Birkat ha-Mazon* for women also appears in the Jerusalem Talmud.[17] However, there is no question at all as to the character of the obligation in the Jerusalem Talmud. According to the Yerushalmi, there can be no doubt that the woman's mitzvah is a biblical one. Now it is true that in cases of disagreement between the Yerusahalmi and the Bavli, we follow the opinion of the Bavli. However, this rule is only valid when the issue is resolved in the Bavli. When, however, a question remains undecided in the Bavli, as in our case, and a decision is given in the Yerushalmi, we usually follow the Yerushalmi. Accordingly, in the subject that we are discussing, the law should be as it appears in the Yerushalmi, i.e., that a woman's obligation to say grace is biblical.

Let us now see why Ravina believes that the woman's obligation in this matter is only rabbinical. Rashi and Tosafot disagree in their analyses of his argument. According to Rashi, Ravina assumes that the commandment cannot be based on the Torah, for the Torah says: "You shall eat and be satisfied and bless the Eternal One, your God, for the good land that He gave you."[18] But we know that the land was divided only between the male members of the tribes of the children of Israel. Women had no share in it. How can they bless God for land that was not given to them? But is it really true that the land of Israel was given only to the males and not to the females?

Let us look at the context in which the blessing for the "good land occurs. For instance: "And remember all the way that the Eternal One, your God, has led you these forty years in the wilderness." Is it possible that these words are addressed only to the male members of the people? Or let us consider the verse: "Keep the commandments of the Eternal One, your God, to walk in His ways and to fear Him. For the Eternal One, your God, brings you into the good land, etc." Is it possible that

16. Or Zarua on Rosh, Megillah 4a.
17. Yerushalmi, Berakhot 3:3.
18. Deuteronomy 8:10.

only the men are required to keep God's commandments, or that women are not included in the passage regarding God's bringing them to the land of promise?

Immediately after these verses follow the words: "And you shall eat and be satisfied and bless the Eternal One, your God, for the good land that He gave you." And the Bible continues: "Beware, lest you forget the Eternal One, your God." Undoubtedly all these verses are directed to the entire people of Israel. God led all the people of Israel; so too the responsibility for the keeping of the Torah rested on all. Even though the land was shared out only to the men for agricultural purpose (so as to avoid the possibility of too much land accumulating in the possession of a few tribes through intertribal marriages), the land in its entirety was God's gift to all the children of Israel. The land of Israel served all the Jewish people. Thus women have to thank God for the "good land" with no less sincerity than men.

Tosafot offers a different explanation of Ravina's position. The grace after meals includes words of thanks "for the covenant that You have sealed in our flesh and for your Torah that You have taught us". According to Tosafot, neither of these phrases applies to women. The "covenant sealed in our flesh" is the circumcision. But this excludes women. So too does the recalling of the "Torah that You have taught us", since women are not commanded to study the Torah. While it is true that the sign of the covenant is visible only on the male body, we must wonder once again whether it is possible that God concluded His covenant only with the men and not with the whole people of Israel, including women no less than men. It is true that women are not commanded to study Torah, but are they not still part of the Jewish people to whom the Torah was given? They are Jews because of the Torah!

From the interpretations of Rashi and Tosafot, we learn that Ravina's problem arose on the basis of the social status of women in his day; as if the essential part of the people were its male members, and women were a kind of auxiliary, needed to maintain the people. This would be in agreement with the Talmudic saying that "women are a people by themselves", as if they were outside the main body of the children of Israel. As we saw above, the problem posed by Ravina was not finally resolved, and according to the *Shulhan Arukh*, women's obligation remains in doubt. However, it would seem to us that today we have every right to follow those halakhic authorities (see above) according to whom the duty of women to say grace after the meal is as biblical as that of men. The social status of women has changed fundamentally. There is no doubt today that women are part of the Jewish people no less than men. The covenant was concluded with the Jewish people, and the land and the Torah were given to all of the Jewish people.

Women Saying Zimun

According to a *baraita* in Tractate Berakhot, women *bentsh mezuman* (i.e., three woman who eat together introduce their *Birkat ha-Mazon* with the special formula that is used also by men).[19] Tosafot comments: "This was never practiced." The phrase in the *baraita* suggests that women are obligated to do so. Tosafot justifies the absence of the practice by saying that the statement that women *bentsh mezuman* may also be understood as meaning that women need do so only if they wish. It is, however, rather difficult to uphold this interpretation, for another Talmudic passage says that all are obligated to *zimun* (if at least three persons have eaten together), and the Talmud interprets "all" as including women, quoting as proof the *baraita* mentioned above to the effect that women say grace in the form of *zimun.*

If this is intended to prove the law that *all* are *obligated* to practice *zimun*, then Tosafot's interpretation that women may do so if they wish cannot hold. Nevertheless, Tosafot insists that *zimun* is not an obligation for women. Notwithstanding the phrase *hakol hayyavim* ("all are obligated"), Tosafot still insists that the meaning is that *zimun* is available for women but is not a duty. Other opinions insist that the words "all are obligated" are to be taken literally, meaning "it is a duty to do so.". This opinion is supported by the Rambam (Maimonides), who writes: "Women … are obligated to say *Birkat ha-Mazon*," and further on in the same passage: "All are obligated to *zimun* as they are obligated

19. Berakhot 45b.

to say the blessing after their meal."[20]

It is worth noting that according to those who maintain that *zimun* is a duty, the matter is not dependent on the question, discussed earlier, of whether the woman's grace obligation is rabbinical or biblical. As we saw, according to Maimonides, the problem raised by Ravina was never resolved and, as Maimonides states, the question remains open. It may very well be that Ravina is right and a woman's obligation is only rabbinical. Nevertheless, according to the Rambam, women are also responsible for *zimun*, since they are obligated, whether biblically or rabbinically, to say *Birkat ha-Mazon*. It would seem, then, that Tosafot and Rashi force themselves to give the phrase "all are obligated" the unconvincing meaning "all may" in order to justify the absence of the practice of *zimun* in their time.

Inclusion of Women in Zimun with Men

The *baraita* discussed in the preceding section concludes with the words "but not together with slaves because of moral looseness [in such a joint company]." This seems to indicate that women may well do *Zimun* together with male Jews, for it is unlikely that such an association will lead to the looseness feared when in the company of slaves. Indeed, the Rosh writes in one of his responsa: "Women fulfill their duty by the *Zimun* of men, since they are sitting together for the meal. If women say *Zimun* by themselves, how much more do they fulfill their duty through the *Zimun* of men?"[21] Of course, the Rosh holds that women have the *duty* to do *Zimun* for themselves, and therefore it is understandable that in his view they may do *Zimun* together with men if they eat together with them.

It is somewhat surprising that the *Shulhan Arukh*, which rules that women may do *Zimun* but are not obligated to, should nevertheless rule "that women eating together with men are obligated and fulfill their duty through our *Zimun*." This agrees with the opinion of another

20. Hilkhot Berakhot 5:6.
21. Hagahot Oshri, Berakhot, chap. 7:4.

halakhic authority, who writes: "Even though *Zimun* is not obligatory for women, yet together with men it is a duty."[22] The various sources indicate that women are to be included with three men for *Zimun*. There is a great surprise in the decision of Rabbi Judah ha-Kohen, who taught that women should be included in a *Zimun* of men.[23] He seems to indicate that there is no need for three women, even one woman may be included. All the authorities speak of inclusion with three men, whose responsibility to say *Zimun* is independent of the number of women to be joined with them. The question now before us is: what may we infer for the women of our time from the various opinions we have mentioned?

There is no doubt that women today may pray in *Zimun*; according to others they are even obligated to do so.

As for their inclusion in the *Zimun* with men, we have learned that if they have their meals together they are obligated to *Zimun* (whether the *Zimun* among themselves is a duty or a choice of their own). The question remains: can women be counted among the required three persons together with one or two men? We meet with a number of reasons against this. Some say that it should not be done because of fear of *peritzut*, i.e., sexual looseness of behavior. We have quoted this phrase from the passage in the Talmud stating that women should not say *Zimun* together with slaves (who are obligated to observe all the *mitzvot* that women have to observe) because it may lead to *peritzut*. The very fact that *peritzut* is mentioned in connection with slaves indicates that it need not be feared in a *Zimun* with Jews. Nevertheless, there are those who insist that women are not to be included in the quorum of three Jews for *Zimun* because such an association may lead to *peritzut*.

Most remarkable is the argument of Rabbenu Nissim (Ran). He maintains that women are obligated to read the Megillah. He is also of the opinion that they may read it in public and even be included in a minyan of ten. Why then can they not be included in *Zimun* to make up the required number of three? And now comes the Ran's surprising answer:

22. Orah Hayyim 199:7.
23. *Tur*, Orah Hayyim 199.

> *Zimun* has a special version that is not used otherwise. If you now include a woman in order to justify *Zimun*, her presence becomes noticeable and there is reason to anticipate *peritzut*. However, if three men are taking part in the meal, *Zimun* is required because of them; in which case women may join in *Zimun* because their participation is not significant. But in the case of Megillah, there is no change whatever in the blessings and the reading because of the inclusion of women. No attention of men is then directed at them. There is no reason to fear *peritzut*.[24]

Even more surprising is Rashi's view. According to Rabbenu Jonah, Rashi explains the statement of the Mishnah that one should not do *Zimun* with women (note, as indicated earlier, that it is said only about joining together with slaves, but nevertheless is applied to men in general) by saying: "Women should not be included in *Zimun* [with men, because of *peritzut*], not even with their husbands, because to be in company with women is not nice."[25] This, obviously, has nothing to do with the reason of possible *peritzut*, which would be utterly meaningless together with one's husband.

Most revealing is a passage in Tosafot.[26] Assuming that women's obligation to say grace after meals is biblical, why should they not be able to perform the mitzvah even for men? The generally accepted principle is that anyone who is obligated to do a mitzvah can perform it for another person who is equally obligated. Explains Tosafot: "A man who does it for another man is different; he is more important [than a woman], or else, because for many, the matter would appear as degrading." Tosafot's words clarify the true reason for the opinions quoted above. Undoubtedly, the reasons given are not based on the Talmudic sources. They originate in the social status of the women of those days. The woman here is still in what we have called her nonpersonal status, lacking the recognition of her personal humanity

24. Ran on Megillah 19b.

25. This passage is not found in the text of Rashi included with the Talmud. See Beit Yosef, Orah Hayyim 199.

26. Sukkah 38a, s.v., *b'emet amru*.

and dignity. The resulting time-conditioned opinions are forced upon the original Talmudic texts. Undoubtedly, the halakhic authorities who utilized these ideas to oppose the participation of women in *Birkat ha-Mazon* together with men were right in their own time. But nowadays, it would be absurd to say that the awareness of their presence because of the *Zimun* formula might lead to *peritzut* or that they must not be included in *Zimun* together with men because the association with them is improper or because men are in higher esteem than women. None of this need concern us.

Only one difficulty still requires our attention. Following the statement that the wife may say *Birkat ha-Mazon* for her husband, it is said that "condemnation is due the man whose wife says the blessing on his behalf." Does this mean that the wife of an ignorant Jew who cannot say grace is not permitted to help him? Or that people who are dining together with family and friends and wish to honor the hostess or another woman in their company are not allowed to do so? The condemnation due a husband whose wife says the blessing for him refers to a specific situation. Explains Rashi, he deserves condemnation either because he did not learn or because if he did learn, he "insults his God by appointing a representative [to say grace for him]." The first reason applies where the wife always performs the mitzvah for her husband. Then, indeed, the husband deserves severe criticism for not wanting to learn how to say the *berakhah*. As for Rashi's second reason, today we would have to say that not allowing the wife to say the blessing after the meal because as a woman she is unworthy of doing so would not be an insult to the Creator, but to the woman whom He created.

Summing up our discussion:

1. Women have every right, and maybe even the duty, to join together among themselves for *Zimun*.

2. We ought to follow the ruling of the Rosh that women fulfill their duty for *Zimun* when they take their meals together with men. As the Rosh formulates it, since they do say *Zimun* among themselves, there is all the more reason for them to fulfill it through the *Zimun* of men.

3. There is every justification for the opinion of Rabbi Judah ha-Kophen, who ruled that even only one woman was to be included in

Zimun and counted to make up the required number of three.

4. We might also accept the opinion of the Rabad, the Ran, and the Rashba that women's obligation to say *Birkat ha-Mazon* is biblical, especially since this is also the teaching of the Jerusalem Talmud. Since this is so, women may well act on behalf of others, female or male.

4. SAYING KIDDUSH AND READING THE MEGILLAH

Strangely enough, as we shall see, the subjects of saying *Kiddush* and reading the Megillah are closely related in the halakhic discussion. The Talmud clearly states that even though *Kiddush* is a *mitzvah aseh she-ha-zeman geramah*, i.e., a commandment dependent on time sequence, women are biblically obligated to say *Kiddush*. Explains Rava: Of the Shabbat the Torah says, "Remember it" and also "Keep it." The two are related to each other. Thus we conclude that he who is obligated to do the one must also do the other. But "to remember" refers to the recitation of the *Kiddush*. We conclude therefore that he who is obligated to keep the Shabbat is also obligated to say *Kiddush*. Since women have to observe the Shabbat no less than men, they have to remember the Shabbat day just as men do. This is the law that is generally accepted on the basis of Rava's explanation.[27] So states, for instance, the *Tur*: "Men and women are equally to say the *Kiddush* of the day."[28] No one disagrees with this.

If followed up, the law has rather important halakhic consequences for the form in which *Kiddush* may be practiced. The *Bet Yosef*, commenting on the ruling of the *Tur*, quotes the *Kol Bo* as follows: "Since women have the same biblical obligation to say *Kiddush* as men, therefore they may fulfill this obligation also for men [i.e., recite *Kiddush* on behalf of men]." There is little doubt that the same conclusion follows from Rashi's explanation in the case of reading the Megillah. In the Talmud it is ruled: "All are obligated regarding the reading of the Megillah. All are religiously qualified [*kesharim*] to read the [Megillah]."[29] When it is

27. Berakhot 20b.
28. Orah Hayyim 271.
29. Arakhin 3a.

asked who is included in the word "all," the answer is that "all" includes women. Explains Rashi: Women are themselves obligated; and women are also qualified to read it for men, i.e., men fulfill their obligation when women read on their behalf. Quite clearly, Rashi intends to explain the connection between the two sentences "All are obligated" and "All are qualified," meaning: Since women have the obligation, they also have the right to do so on behalf of men. This is in keeping with the general principle according to which a person who has the duty to fulfill a mitzvah has the authority to enact it on behalf of another person who is under the same obligation. It is obvious that the same rule applies to the mitzvah of *Kiddush*. Since the commandment of *Kiddush* for women is of the same biblical force as that for men, women have the right to say *Kiddush* on behalf of men. And indeed it is so stated in the *Shulhan Arukh*: "Women may perform the *Kiddush* on behalf of men because they are obligated to do it just as men."[30]

All this seems to be quite simple and clear, in keeping with generally valid halakhic principles. Yet, to our surprise, the Bah disagrees with the *Shulhan Arukh*'s ruling. Commenting on the *Tur*,[31] he maintains that the decision of the *Shulhan Arukh* in the case of *Kiddush* contradicts its ruling on the reading of the Megillah. In section 689, says the Bah, the *Shulhan Arukh* maintains that "some say" that women may not read the Megillah on behalf of men, based on the words of the Behag, who disagrees with Rashi's view that women may read the Megillah for men. It is astounding, says the Bah, that the *Shulhan Arukh* should follow Rashi's ruling in the case of *Kiddush*, but accept the opinion of Behag, who disagrees with Rashi, in regard to the Megillah. The Bah concludes that one may not treat *Kiddush* and Megillah differently, supporting his decision by adding that the Rashal ruled as he does. It would seem, then, that the Behag's ruling is the basis for the opinion, stated in the *Shulhan Arukh*, that *yesh omrim* ("some say") that women may not read the Megillah for men. But what is the source of the Behag's opinion?

Tosafot explains that the proof for the Behag's decision is a Tosefta where it is said clearly that "women, slaves, and minor children are free

30. Orah Hayyim 271:2.
31. Ibid.

from the reading of the Megillah."[32] However, the Behag adds to these words: "Even though they are free from reading it, they are obligated to hear it." This, of course, contradicts the plain meaning of what we have quoted from the Mishnah and Gemara in Tractate Arakhin, that all are obligated to read the Megillah and all are (religiously) qualified to read it. As we learned, the word "all" included women.

According to the generally valid halakhic principle, if a Tosefta is in disagreement with a Talmudic ruling, the Talmudic source prevails. Tosafot, wishing to defend the opinion of the Behag, makes a tortuous effort to reconcile the Behag's teaching with that of the Talmud. It explains that "the word 'all' includes women" means that "one should not think that women cannot read the Megillah even for women. For that reason it is first said: 'All are obligated to hear the reading of the Megillah, and thus women may read it to women [who are obligated to hear it] like themselves.'" All this is, of course, extremely forced. The same words have different meanings for men and for women. For men they say: "All are obligated to read the Megillah; therefore, they may fulfill the mitzvah for each other." But for women the meaning is: "All women are obligated to hear the Megillah read; consequently, women may read it for women." In itself this is difficult to accept. But it is even more difficult to agree with the second part of the explanation: since women are obligated to listen to the Megillah, they have the right to read it to women. This is a logical non sequitur. It does not follow from the fact that women should hear the Megillah that therefore they may read it to other women.

If we now return to the starting point of our discussion, we must note that there is no contradiction between the rulings of the *Shulhan Arukh* in regard to *Kiddush* and Megillah. In the case of *Kiddush*, the halakhic authorities agree that women are obligated to say it and, therefore, may also say it on behalf of men. However, in the laws of Megillah the Bahag holds that women are not obligated to read it and therefore cannot do so for men. Consequently, the Bah's equation between *Kiddush* and Megillah is not valid. His *Humrah*, i.e., his suggested "strictness" about *Kiddush*, is without foundation. Here is the concluding comment of the

32. Arakhin, 3a, s.v., *l'atuyi nashim*.

Taz, the son-in-law of the Bah, on the subject:

> There is no contradiction in the words of the *Shulhan Arukh*. The law of *Kiddush* is unlike the law of reading the Megillah. For in the case of the Megillah there are opinions that women should say the blessing not over the reading of the Megillah but over the hearing of the Megillah being read… therefore, surely it is not proper that *l'khathila* [i.e., ruling *ab initio*], women should read it for men. However, here [i.e., in the case of *Kiddush*] all agree that there is no difference between men and women. Thus, it is proper that women may perform the *Kiddush* also for the sake of men. The Rashal and my father-in-law, of blessed memory, ruled that here, too [i.e., the law of *Kiddush*], women may not say it for men, just as in the case of Megillah. But this is not convincing at all.[33]

It would seem to us that there is additional proof for the words of the Taz. The *Shulhan Arukh* brings the ruling of the *yesh omrim*, i.e., that "some say" that women have no right to read the Megillah for men, which seems to be in accordance with the Behag's decision, but it is evident that he does not fully accept the Behag's opinion. According to the Behag, as we noted, women are not obligated to read the Megillah themselves but only to hear its reading. This being so, it is obvious that they cannot do the reading for men. But the *Shulhan Arukh* states clearly that women's obligation is to read and not just to listen to the reading. That is why the *Shulhan Arukh* brings the opinion of the Behag as *yesh omrim*, "some say," which means that the opinion is not fully binding. If you disagree with the Behag and have found that women are obligated to read the Megillah, then you rule that they may also do so on behalf of men. Why then does the *Shulhan Arukh* quote the view of the Behag at all? At this point the Taz's comment is clarified. He is saying that since in the case of the Megillah there is an opinion that women may not act on behalf of men, we are *mahmir* (strict) about the matter and do not allow women to fulfill this commandment for men. But this is not the rule on all occasions. The Taz adds the word

33. Orah Hayyim 271:2.

l'khathila as a generally valid practice; however, if *be-diavad*, i.e., if it happened – perhaps mistakenly, or for some other reason present in a given situation – that a woman did read the Megillah for a man, his duty was fulfilled by her reading on his behalf. Unquestionably the Taz's ruling is correct: *Kiddush* is not to be compared to the reading of the Megillah. Thus, the original principle in the case of saying *Kiddush* remains binding: since women are obligated to say *Kiddush* just as men, they may perform this duty on behalf of men.

Let us now clarify the woman's obligation regarding the reading of the Megillah. We noted above the opinion of Rashi, who, basing himself on the discussion of the subject in Tractate Arakhin, stated that since women are obligated to read the Megillah, they may also do it for men. This is also the view of Maimonides, who holds as follows: "All are obligated to read it, men and women, etc."[34] Then he continues: "Whether one reads it himself or hears it from the reader, he has fulfilled his duty; but only if he hears it from one who himself is obligated to read it. Therefore, if the reader was a minor or a mentally disturbed person, he who hears it from him has not done his duty." Since Maimonides states that women are obligated to read the Megillah but does not mention women when, soon afterwards, he lists those who are not fit for the task of acting on behalf of others, it proves that women may read the Megillah for men. This is also how the Magid Mishneh, commenting on Maimonides' words, interprets his meaning. Rabbenu Nissim (Ran) is of the opinion that women have the right to read the Megillah for men and may even be included with men in the minyan required for public reading. "For how could it be that women may read it for men but should not be included with them in the minyan? Undoubtedly, they may be included."[35] The Rosh quotes the opinion of Rashi as well as that of the Behag: the *Bet Yosef* explains that the Rosh is leaning towards the view of the Behag and is *mahmir* in the matter.[36] The Mordekhai quotes the Rabyah, who follows the

34. Yad ha-Hazaka, Megillah 1:1.
35. Megillah 2, conclusion.
36. *Tur*, Orah Hayyim 689.

ruling of the Behag.[37]

We saw that the *Shulhan Arukh* quotes the opinion of the Behag as *yesh omrim*, "some say." The very fact that he rules that women are obligated to read the Megillah and not, like the Behag, that their duty is only to listen to its reading, proves that his acceptance of the Behag's view is only partial. His own view is that women may fulfill the duty of reading on behalf of men. He quotes the Behag as *yesh omrim* as a concession *le-humra* (to a stricter view), which does not require adherence in all situations (as we have explained above). However, for the sake of pure Halakhah, let us review the original sources on this subject once again. Undoubtedly, the Tosefta on which the Behag relies for his view contradicts the Talmudic teaching. All the efforts to eliminate the contradiction are unconvincing. The explanation that the statement in the Talmud, that women are qualified to read the Megillah means qualified to read it for women, is forced. What is worse is the fact that this alone is not enough. What about the statement that all are obligated to read the Megillah, including women? The answer has been to correct the text and read it as saying: "All are obligated to hear the Megillah." These explanations cannot be accepted. Why indeed should women not be obligated to read the Megillah just as men?

This is how the ruling about women's obligation in this matter is formulated by Rabbi Joshua ben Levi: "Women are obligated to read the Megillah, for they too were in that miracle."[38] Explains the Rashbam: "Indeed it was so. The main part of the Purim miracle was due to the woman Esther." Of course, the words "for they too" do not say that women had the greatest share in the miracle. Therefore Tosafot explains Rabbi Joshua ben Levi's statement as meaning: "Women were in danger of being killed together with men."[39] And they were saved by the same miracle. Surely, this ought to be enough to obligate women to read the Megillah just as men. This is what Rabbi Joshua ben Levi is saying.

True, the Mordekhai (as above; see also *Bet Yosef* as above) believes that the view that women are obligated only to hear the reading is

37. Megillah 1.
38. Megillah 4a.
39. Ibid; see Tosafot, s.v., *she-af hen hayu be-oto ha-nes*.

supported by the passage in the Yerushalmi, where Bar Kapara says: "One has to read it [i.e., the Megillah] before women and children."[40] With all due respect to the Mordekhai, the passage only indicates that the educational level of women was like that of children. They were unable to read the Megillah by themselves; therefore it was necessary to read it for them. The proof for this is found immediately after the words of Bar Kapara, where we are told the Rabbi Joshua ben Levi would assemble his children and the members of his household and read the Megillah to them. We know that Rabbi Joshua ben Levi holds that women are obligated to read the Megillah themselves just as men. Why, then, did he read for them? Quite clearly, with the women as with his children, he was attempting, for educational purpose, to introduce them to the reading of the Megillah.

There is another attempt to disqualify women from reading the Megillah for men by the Magen Avraham. On the opinion quoted in the *Shulhan Arukh* as "some say" (see above), the Magen Avraham comments: "One may not compare the reading of the Megillah to the lighting of the Hanukkah candles, which women perform also on behalf of men. The reading of the Megillah is different. It is like the reading of the Torah, which should not be done by women because of the dignity of the assembled congregation. And since women should not do it in public, neither should they do it for individual men. For we should not make a distinction."[41] Of all this there is not even a hint in the Talmudic sources. There is little doubt that time-conditioned attitudes and opinions regarding women were forced upon the clear teachings of the Talmud and upon the original meaning of authentic Halakhah. It was all justified at that time. It was the time-conditioned truth. However, in our day it is essential that we return to the original Talmudic sources without forced explanations, and rely, in matters of halakhic practice, on Rashi, the Rambam, and the Ran.

Only one more point remains that still may require clarification. The *Divrei Hamudot* remarks that even though women may recite the *Kiddush* for men, a husband whose wife does it for him will be in the

40. Megillah 2:5.
41. Ibid.

category of which the Talmud says: "May a curse descend on the man whose wife says the blessing on his behalf."[42] This is indeed surprising. The Talmud quotes that *baraita* in order to prove that women may do *mitzvot* which are obligatory for them for all who are under the same obligation. How is it possible, then, to say that a curse will descend upon all who permit a mitzvah to be done by a woman on their behalf? Is it inconceivable that an *am ha-aretz* (ignorant Jew) may occasionally be in need of some help in saying the *Kiddush* or the *Birkat ha-Mazon*? It would seem that a man is exposed to such severe criticism only in the case of his wife saying the *berakhah* for him. But it applies if it is done as a continuous practice; i.e., the husband not only does not know how to say the *berakhah* but does not intend to learn it.

As we saw, Rashi offers two reasons to explain the *baraita*'s statement that such practice is rejected: first, the husband has not learned; and second, if he has learned, he insults his Creator by appointing representatives "like those." Quite clearly we have every right to reject Rashi's second reason. Nowadays the very words are an insult to a creation of the Creator, the wife. As for his first reason, it is, of course, as valid today as it was in Talmudic times. The task of the wife is certainly not to replace her husband in the saying of the required blessings because he refuses to learn them. This would be objectionable as a permanent practice. But there is no reason whatsoever why in our days husband and wife may not alternate from Shabbat to Shabbat in the saying of the *Kiddush*. It would be our expression of respect for the wife and mother.

5. TALMUDIC AND HALAKHIC EFFORTS TO IMPROVE THE WIFE'S STATUS IN RELATIONSHIP TO HER HUSBAND

Undoubtedly the laws of marriage and divorce grant the husband a degree of power that often has severe consequences for the wife. Our sages (*Hazal*) were aware of this and attempted, with great courage and sincere concern, to introduce solutions to many of the problems it

42. Berakhot 20b, note 35.

caused. We intend to present some of them here. They are all halakhic innovations.

In the case of giving a *get* to one's wife, the Torah commands: "He [the husband] shall write her a divorce document and give it into her hands."[43] Of course, it is hardly possible for every husband to write the *get* himself. The writing of a *get* requires a special technique of which most husbands are incapable. Therefore our teachers interpreted the word *ve-katab*, "and he shall write," as meaning that the husband has to pay the fee of the *sofer* (professional scribe). The law is stated clearly in a mishnah.[44] Nevertheless, after some time, the custom changed. Instead of the husband, it was the wife who usually paid the fee. The Talmud explains that the rabbis gave this duty to the wife so that her divorce would not be unduly delayed.[45] Apparently husbands who did not wish to pay a *sofer* to write a *get* would simply leave home without divorcing their wives. Having no *get*, the wife would become an *agunah*, a woman who had no husband but was still legally married, and thus was unable to marry another man. In order to avoid such injustices, the rabbis ruled that the wife should pay for the writing of the *get*.

The decision was obviously not easy for the rabbis. It went against the law of the Torah. There is even a Talmudic opinion stating that this deviation from the biblical rule might be sufficient to invalidate all divorces, since the Torah ordered "and he shall write" and here it is she who is writing it for him. Rava, however, found a reason that justified the deviation. In monetary matters, we work with the principle *hefker bet din hefker*, i.e., expropriation by the duly established rabbinical court (of former times) is valid. Thus, it is possible that the rabbis conveyed to the husband ownership of the money the wife spent on the writing of the *get*. In essence, however, this was a change of a biblical law in order to protect the wife. Since, however, protecting another human being against an act of injustice is also a Torah obligation, one might say that in this case the rabbis changed a biblical rule with the force of another biblical rule that they applied for the sake of the wife against

43. Deuteronomy 24:1.
44. Bava Batra 167a.
45. Ibid. 168a.

a husband who was not willing to fulfill his obligation as commanded by the Torah.

Rather different is the practical leniency for the sake of the wife when the witnesses to the writing of the *get* are illiterate. In general, the rule was that only witnesses who were able to read and write were allowed to testify on any document. Yet, in the case of divorce documents, Rabbi Simeon ben Gamliel ruled that "with witnesses who cannot read, one reads for them and they sign. And with witnesses who are unable to sign, one scratches the shape of the letters of their names on the paper, which they can fill in afterwards with ink."[46]

It would seem that this latter law, where the witnesses just fill in ink in the places prepared for them, goes much further than the one when the text of the *get* is read to the witnesses who can, at least, sign with their own handwriting. These arrangements, which are in fact contrary to important laws of adequate testimony, were instituted, says Rabbi Elazar, so that the daughters of Israel would not become *agunot*. The reason was that the husband might want to leave urgently for another land or a distant place. If no other witnesses were immediately available, he might depart without divorcing his wife. She would then be an *agunah*, "anchored" to a man who in fact no longer lived with her as a husband.

These are only a few examples of this category. We shall now consider the cases where the rabbis limited or even removed the power the husband received by the act of *kiddushin*, the legal espousal of his wife. As is well known, the husband has to give the *get* to his wife only of his own free will. But our sages saw that, at times, there were marriages where it was, indeed, impossible to leave the wife under the control of her husband. The Mishnah lists a number of cases that prevent a woman from continuing married life with her husband: if the husband suffers from a certain illness (*shehin*) that does not allow him to lead a normal life with his wife, or if his work attaches a bad odor to his body, or if he has a bad odor caused by certain bodily ailments related to the nose or the mouth (all this was the case in mishnaic times).[47] In

46. Gittin 19b.
47. Ketubot 77a.

such cases, the husband was compelled until he was willing to say *rotzeh ani*, "Yes, I am ready to divorce my wife of my free will." Here is not the place to enter into a detailed discussion of such cases. Suffice it to note that even though, according to the Torah, a *get* may not be given against the husband's will, the wife in the situations related above could not be expected to continue her marriage, and in consequence our sages found ways to force the husband to give a *get* of his own free will.[48]

The principle of *kofin oto ad she-yomar rotzeh ani*, "one compels him until he says that he is willing to give the *get*," was used on many occasions, not only in the cases listed in the Mishnah. The Amoraim applied it often to their understanding of the need in the cases before them. For instance, a woman once came before Rav Nahman, demanding a *get* from her husband.[49] Her reason was that her husband was incapable of begetting children. Rav Nahman initially replied, You are not commanded!" meaning, "As a woman, you are not obligated to produce offspring [the obligation, according to the Torah, is only on men, not on women]. Therefore your demand for a *get* is not valid." But the woman could not be so easily dismissed. She said to Rav Nahman: "Does this woman not need a cane for her hand and a spade for her burial?" She was, in fact, saying to Rav Nahman, "Even though I was not commanded to give birth to children, will I not be in need, in my old age, of sons and daughters on whom to lean, and when I die, to bury me?" The ruling of Rav Nahman was spontaneous: "When like this, we certainly compel," meaning, "In a case like this we certainly compel the husband until he is ready to give the *get* freely." Such a decision requires from the *dayan* (rabbinical judge) a great deal of courage to accept the responsibility and to rule according to the principle that "the *dayan* must consider only what his eyes see."

Another category of halakhot shows the extent to which our sages were willing to go in *halakhic* innovation in order to protect the vital well-being of the wife against the power that the form of *kiddushin* provides for the husband. In certain cases they were even willing to annul

48. E.g., Maimonides justifies this apparently self-contradictory procedure in Laws of Divorce 2:5 and 2:20. There are, of course, other explanations.

49. Yevamot 65b.

the validity of the *kiddushin* and thus dissolve the marriage retroactively, freeing the wife from the need for a divorce. The origin of such a ruling is found in Tractate Gittin.[50] According to the *din* (law), one could divorce one's wife by sending her a *get* through a *shaliah* (representative). At the same time, the husband could withdraw the authorization that he gave his *shaliah* or simply annul the *get*. Regrettably, he could do this even without the knowledge of his representative or of the wife. This could lead to very serious consequences for the wife. The husband could go to any Beth Din (rabbinical court) and declare that he was annulling the *get* or cancelling his representative. Neither the *shaliah* nor the wife had to be informed of the cancellation. The wife would still receive the *get*. Considering herself divorced, she might then remarry. Her second marriage would be invalid. She would be obliged to leave her second husband, but, having lived with another man, she was not permitted to return to her first husband.

In order to protect the wife, Rabban Gamliel the Elder introduced a *takkanah* (improvement on the law) by forbidding the husband to cancel his representative or the *get* without informing the representative or the wife, whichever the case might require. But now the Gemara discusses the question: what happens if a husband disregards the *takkanah* of Rabban Gamliel and withdraws his representative or the *get* before a Beth Din in another place? Says Rabbi Simeon ben Gamliel: "He can neither relent, nor can he add anything to the conditions attached to the *get*. Otherwise, what authority is left to the Beth Din?" against which the argument is raised: How is that possible: according to the Torah this *get* is invalid [i.e., it was cancelled by the husband before it reached the wife], and because otherwise what authority is left to the Beth Din, we allow a married woman to anyone [who is willing to marry her]?" The question is answered: "One espouses a wife according to rabbinical determination, and the rabbis removed the validity of the *kiddushin*." The *kiddushin* is enacted with the words: "I am espousing you in accordance with the law of Moses and Israel." But our sages established the rule that we must not annul a *get* without the knowledge of the wife. The husband who nevertheless does so violates an obligation

50. Gittin 33a.

than he took upon himself as binding for the act of marriage. Thus, the *kiddushin* becomes invalid retroactively.

It is important to note that the retroactive annulment of the marriage was used not only when the husband violated a known and established rabbinical rule but even spontaneously, according to the need of the situation. The Talmud relates an incident that occurred in a place called Narash.[51] A man married a minor. Such marriages could be dissolved by the girl when she reached the halakhically legal majority at the age of twelve. Very often another act of *kiddushin* would be arranged that would be fully binding. In this case, the girl having reached the required age, the husband brought her under a *huppah* (marriage canopy) with the intention of marrying her in accordance with the law valid between grown-ups. However, another man anticipated this, took her away, and gave her *kiddushin*. According to the law of the Torah the marriage to the minor had no biblical validity, whereas the *kiddushin* of the second man was fully valid. Yet the rabbis took the wife away from the second man and returned her to the man who was her husband in her minority. This was done without requiring a *get* from the second man. The rabbis invalidated the girl's marriage to him. The explanation given is: "He acted improperly, so we too treat him improperly and invalidate his *kiddushin*." Once again the same method of rabbinical enforcement was used.

There was, however, a great difference between the two cases. In the example that we have discussed earlier, there existed a *takkanah* of Rabban Gamliel the Elder. To observe the arrangement made by Rabban Gamliel was one of the conditions included in the act of *kiddushin*. To violate it was a violation of one of the major responsibilities that the husband-to-be took upon himself. Thus the marriage became retroactively invalid. The case of Narash was rather different. There was no rabbinical *takkanah* attached to the marriage act as a condition that was violated. But something much more important is included in "the laws of Moses and Israel,", namely, proper moral behavior. If the husband violates it, he violates a vital condition of the marriage that he undertook to keep.

51. Yevamot 90b.

With equal courage, Rava proceeded to validate a *get* and permit the woman to remarry, even though the *get* was invalid according to the original law of the Torah. Let us consider the case in detail. According to the halakhic principle of *oness rahmana patrei*, if a person undertook an obligation with the proviso that it was dependent on a condition he had to fulfill, and circumstances beyond his control made it impossible for him to fulfill the condition, he was adjudged to have met the terms of his obligation. For instance, assume that a husband, on the eve of his departure on a long journey, hands his wife a *get* that will take effect only if he does not return within a certain time. In accordance with this principle, he is considered to have fulfilled his obligation if he set out on the return trip but was prevented from arriving before the deadline because of a flood on the road or some other circumstance beyond his control. Since he is then considered as having returned in time, the *get* loses its validity, and the marriage remains in full force.

Now, Rava came along and, on the strength of his own reasoning, declared: *Ein ones be-gittin*; i.e., in cases of divorce we must not pay attention to the effects of intervening superior forces or circumstances.[52] In other words, if the husband does not return at the appointed time, no matter what the cause might have been, he has in fact not returned and the *get* becomes valid, as was stipulated. What was the basis for Rava's surprising ruling against a well-established halakhic principle?

The explanation given is that Rava acted out of consideration of the effects the original law would have on two kinds of women: those who are chaste, and those whose sexual values are unreliable. If the husband does not return, the chaste wife will always assume that he was prevented from returning by something that was beyond his control. Therefore, she will always believe that the *get* is invalid and that she is a married woman. The sexually loose woman will always maintain the opposite, that her husband never intended to return and thus her divorce is valid. In the first case, the wife becomes an *agunah* even if the husband does not intend to return, but if the *get* was valid, she would be free to remarry. In the second case, the wife will always consider herself divorced and free to marry whomever she pleases, even though

52. Ketubot 2b.

the husband may want to return but is prevented from doing so by circumstances beyond his control, and in this eventuality the *get* is invalid and the wife remains a married woman.

Because of these considerations, Rava decided to invalidate the otherwise ruling principle that overwhelming circumstances release a person from the consequences of non-fulfillment of the condition he agreed to. Thus, a husband who gives his wife a *get* that will only take effect if he does not return at a certain time should know that if he does not return, regardless of the reason, the *get* becomes valid, and he and his wife are divorced. In light of this, it is natural to ask how a *get* that is invalid according to Torah law can be declared valid by the rabbis, so that a marriage is dissolved. Once again the answer is the one found in the tractate of Kiddushin: everyone who marries a woman does it by the formula "according to the law of Moses and Israel." Since Rava's ruling has been incorporated into the law of Moses and Israel, the rabbis had the right to render a marriage invalid by annulling it retroactively.

One of the most surprising rabbinical decisions was the ruling concerning testimony about the death of a husband. Let us assume that a husband went on a long journey and only one witness testified that he is dead. The witness's testimony is accepted even if it is based on what he heard from another person, even when the witness is a woman reporting what she heard from another woman or from a male or female slave. On this basis, the wife is considered a widow and permitted to remarry.

This rabbinical ruling is a deviation from the law of the Torah in all its phases. According to the Torah, two male witnesses are required in order to establish a fact in a Beth Din by testimony. In addition, women are not accepted as witnesses; and testimony based on hearsay is not accepted. How could our sages depart from these laws of the Torah? The answer is as follows: if the woman should remarry and the husband then returned, the wife would still have been married to him when she married her second husband, and thus would have committed adultery. Since the law would demand that she leave her second husband, but not permit her to return to the first one, she would be extremely careful about relying on testimony that is not normally admitted. However, the problem is not fully solved, for the question remains: why did the rabbis initially allow her to remarry on the strength of such questionable testimony? If they had insisted on two valid witnesses, there would not have been any need to rely in the end on the wife's conscientiousness when remarrying. The final answer is: "In order to protect the woman from becoming an *agunah*, they were lenient in this case."[53] They realized that it might be impossible to find two qualified witnesses who actually saw the husband die or dead, and in that case the wife would be bound for life to an absent husband. Our sages acted in order to protect the wife. (Some of the authorities, among them Tosafot and Maimonides, endeavor to explain the halakhic validity of the deviation from an otherwise generally effective biblical law.)

An important subject that is rather close to the conditions of married life in our own times is the one halakhically known as the case of the *moredet* (rebellious woman). A rebellious woman is a wife who declares that she is unable to submit to her husband sexually. He is strongly displeasing to her. The husband of a *moredet* is compelled to divorce her, but halakhic authorities disagree as to whether this rule is found in the Talmud, or was a later introduction of the *yeshivot* and the sages of the Gaonic period in Babylon.

Maimonides, for instance, maintains that the rule is of Talmudic origin. Here is his formulation: "A wife who refuses to submit to her husband in the sexual act is called *moredet*. We ask her for the reason of her refusal. If her answer is that he has become displeasing to her, we compel the husband to divorce her there and then; she is not like a prisoner of her husband to be forced to submit to one whom she hates."[54] Alfasi, who holds that the rule to compel the husband to divorce does not have its origin in the Talmud, adds: "However, today, in the rabbinical courts in the *yeshivot*, this is how they rule in the case of the *moredet*: when she comes and says, 'I do not want this man, let him give me a *get*,' let him give her a *get* immediately, etc."[55]

There are sources confirming that Rav Hai Gaon and Rabbenu Gershom introduced in the Babylonian *yeshivot* the practice of

53. Yevamot 122a.
54. Ishut 14:8.
55. Rif, Ketubot 63a-b.

compelling the husband to give a *get* in a case of this kind. Other authorities, like the Rashbbam, the Rosh, and Rabbenu Tam, disagree with this approach, excusing their departure from the practice of the Gaonim on the grounds that the latter had instituted their *takkanah* only for their own generation. The same criticism was directed against the opinion of the Alfasi (Rif) quoted earlier. Nachmanides (Ramban) defended the Rif against such criticism in rather strong language. This is how he formulates it:

> What is asserted… that the institution of the *yeshivot* [in Babylon] was intended only for the passing hour [*hora'at sha'ah*], our great teacher [i.e., the Alfasi] had a better knowledge of the *takkanot* of the Gaonim than any of us. His words prove that the Gaonim gave their decision in this matter for the generations to come, etc… it was the practice till the time of the Rif. For five hundred years this arrangement was not moved… as it was known by them in their responsa. You find this expressly in the early responsa of Rabbi Simeon Kayyara and in all the works of the *rishonim* [the early recognized authorities], as well as in those of the *aharonim* [the later authorities], and they were familiar with how these *takkanot* were intended, etc.

One learns from the various sources that one must not judge the case of the *moredet* on the basis of a general, all-comprehensive principle. The deciding authority is obligated to investigate every case as unique of its kind. He must make the effort to understand the "mind of the woman." As one of the authorities expresses it: "Even an *ishah kesherah* [religiously reliable woman] cannot submit to a man who is hated by her." We may add that especially for an *ishah kesherah* it is hardly possible to live with a husband after the intimate bond of the marriage has broken down and mutual understanding has ceased.

For many generations after the conclusion of the Talmud, because of their deep understanding of the serious problems of the wife's well-being, rabbis often used the ruling of "We compel him [to give the *get*] until he himself agrees to do it." In case of need, they even went so far as to annul the legality of the marriage retroactively. In the *Shulhan Arukh*, the Rema writes that it is a sin for a husband to beat his wife, and then quotes the opinion that if he was warned once or twice and did not listen, one compels him to divorce her.[56]

The teaching of the Tashbaz in his responsa deserves special attention.[57] He was asked about a husband whose treatment of his wife caused her to suffer. The Tashbaz continues: "And all know that he is a very hard man. She cannot endure him because of the many quarrels; he also starves her, so that she actually hates life itself." His answer was: "He should let her go and pay her the value of the *ketubah*, for we practice the principle that a 'woman was created for life and not for suffering' [based on the biblical explanation of the name Eve: 'For she was the mother of all living']."[58] The Tashbaz further strengthens his argument by adding: "A person cannot live together with a snake in one basket… quarreling in the house is more difficult to endure than a home without food." Finally, he concludes that in the case before him "one compels the husband until he agrees [to divorce her]."

The Tashbaz does not ignore the fact that some of the later halakhic authorities (*aharonim*) do not agree that the husband can be forced to give a *get*. He adds: "But neither are we to be disregarded. And in a matter that depends on logical consideration, the *dayan* [rabbinical judge] has nothing but what his own eyes see." Undoubtedly, this is the right approach for the halakhic decision, especially in our own days.

Some rabbis objected to the idea of retroactively annulling marriage because of the seriousness of the possible violations of the laws regarding married women. Nevertheless, in every generation from the time of the Babylonian Gaonim almost until our own day, many communities established communal marital regulations the violation of which would lead to retroactive annulment of the marriage. In general this was done with the approval of recognized and highly respected halakhic authorities.[59]

56. Even ha-Ezer 154, 3.

57. Responsa, II. Part. chap. 3.

58. *Ketubot* 61a, citing Genesis 3:20.

59. E.g., A.H. Freimann's *Seder Kiddushin ve-Nissu'in me-Aharei Hatimat ha-Talmud ad Zemanenu;* also M. Elon's *Ha-Mishpat ha-Ivri* 2:20.

If in past generations the problems were so serious that rabbinical sages and communities were compelled to renew the solution of retroactive annulment, how much more serious are the problems today, when there have been fundamental social, educational, and professional changes in the status of the woman! In my work, *Tenai be-Nissu'in u-ve-Get*, I have shown that there are halakhic possibilities to introduce conditions into the *ketubah* (marriage contract) whose violation would bring about the retroactive annulment of the marriage. (I regret to say that my work has not been given serious consideration, and instead all kinds of statements have been made maintaining that my teacher, Rabbi Y. Y. Weinberg, z.l., withdrew the moral support that he gave to the work. I have to declare that in all these statements and rumors there is not the slightest truth.)

It is difficult to understand how the rabbinical authorities of our day can so utterly disregard the humanitarian commitments and important principles of halakhic ethics that guided the halakhic practice of the Talmudic and post-Talmudic sages.

6. THE AGUNAH PROBLEM

The problem of the *agunah*, in the widest sense, has some very serious implications for the status of women in our days. There are numerous cases of unscrupulous husbands misusing their halakhically awarded control over the divorce process. Some men have demanded extortionate sums of money from the wife or her family before agreeing to a divorce. Others have withheld the *get* as a way of forcing a wife to accept an unfair property settlement. Still others, with vicious intent, simply refuse to give a *get*, and abandon their wives without divorcing them.

All this causes a great deal of suffering for wives, especially in Israel, where they may have to wait for years before a divorce is arranged, not necessarily in accordance with strict principles of justice. The problem has different facets, though no less serious, in the Diaspora. While demands for money in return for a *get* come there too, of course, a woman who refuses to submit to blackmail by her husband may instead turn to civil divorce as a solution to the problem. If she does so, and then wishes to marry someone else, she may find a rabbi who is willing to officiate without raising any questions regarding a religious divorce from her previous marriage. Or else, as often happens, she can remarry in a civil ceremony. In both cases, according to Jewish law, she would be an *eshet ish*, a married woman living with another man. Her children, *mamzerim*, would not be allowed to marry into the Jewish community.

Since Talmudic times, no generation has been without problems of this kind. It is our intention to summarize briefly some of those problems and show how rabbis, among them some of the greatest halakhic authorities, struggled to solve them.[60] As we will see, they did so by utilizing the halakhic concept of *tenai be-kiddushin* (conditional marriage).

The practice of conditional marriage existed already in Talmudic times, as is shown by the following story told in the Talmud:[61] In Alexandria, toward the end of the Second Temple period, people would give *kiddushin* to their wives (i.e., legally espouse a woman as wife by giving her an object of value for that purpose). But when the time of their entering into the *huppah* (marriage canopy) arrived, other men would come and take them away (by force) and marry them. The sages intended to declare the children *mamzerim*, since the mothers had been legally married before and the second marriage was invalid. Said Hillel the Elder, "Show me the *ketubah* [original marriage contract] of your mothers." They brought it to him, and it was found written in it: "When you move to my house, you shall be my wife according to the laws of Moses and Israel." Naturally, the sages no longer declared the offspring *mamzerim*, for the condition "when you move into my house" invalidated the act of the first *kiddushin*.

On the basis of contemporary practice, it may be difficult to understand the meaning of this story. Originally, the two phases of

60. The examples reported here are mainly taken from the excellent work of A. Freimann, cited in the preceding note. A comprehensive discussion of the halakhic issues involved will be found in my work. *Tenai bi-Nissu'in u-ve-Get* (Jerusalem: Mosad Harav Kook, 1966 ; 2nd ed. 2008).

61. Bava Mezia 104a.

marriage, *erusin* and *nissu'in*, were separated from each other in time. *Erusin*, normally translated as "engagement," was not an "engagement" in the sense in which the term is understood today. It was *kiddushin*, the actual legal espousal of a person as one's wife by giving her the required object of value and saying, in the presence of two witnesses: "With this ring [or coin or any object of value] I wed you in accordance with the law of Moses and Israel." *Nissu'in*, the ceremony under the *huppah* and the joining of the bride and bridegroom, followed sometime after *erusin*. As a rule, the bride was given twelve months to prepare herself for married life, which started with *nissu'in*. Since that act of "engagement" could take place at any time, in any place, and in the presence of any two witnesses, even without the knowledge of the family or any other public announcement, it often, apparently, was not taken very seriously by the two parties. Either or both might change their minds long before *nisu'in*; the bridegroom might marry another woman or the bride agree to marry another man, even allowing herself to be carried away by force. In the first case, she is deserted by her prospective husband; in the second, she is deserting him. But in both cases, the original act of *erusin* is valid, so she is an *eshet ish*, a legally married woman.

When she is deserted, she becomes an *agunah* and cannot marry another man without a *get*. In the other case, if she lives with another man, both are committing adultery and their children are *mamzerim*. In order to solve this problem, a condition (*tenai*) was introduced into the *ketubah* stating that the *kiddushin* of the *erusin* would take effect only if followed by the appropriate arrangement of the *nissu'in*. In other words, if *nissu'in* did not take place, the act of *kiddushin* became invalid. The woman would then be free, according to Halakhah, to marry another man.

However, the same problem continued to trouble other communities, especially in the East, in Africa, and later on in Italy and other places. Because of the time lapse between the *erusin* and the *nissu'in* and the private nature of *erusin*, there were a great many secret "engagements," the seducing of inexperienced young girls to accept *kiddushin* from all kinds of questionable characters. This happened especially to daughters of well-to-do families. Often these "engagements" were dishonest, intended only for the purpose of exploiting the families.

In order to eliminate this evil, various communities instituted *takkanot* (communal regulations) ordering that *nissu'in*, the union of bride and bridegroom under the *huppah*, should follow immediately upon the *kiddushin* by *erusin*. In time it was found that this was not enough. Thus, further *takkanot*_were introduced requiring that all marriages be supervised by the rabbi of the community, the *mara de-atra*, who would also officiate at the marriage ceremony. In some instances it was prescribed that all marriages had to take place in the presence of a number of communal trustees appointed for that purpose. Later on, the presence of at least ten people was necessary. (In a sense, this is the historical basis for our present practice of *kiddushin* and *huppah* taking place at the same time and in the presence of ten people.) When the prospective bridegroom did not obey these rules, he would be put into *herem* (religious excommunication) or a monetary punishment would be imposed. He might even be put in prison, or given a form of corporal punishment.

But what was to be done in cases where people disobeyed these rulings? The problem became extremely serious after the loss of communal autonomy, when Jewish communities and rabbinical courts were no longer able to enforce punishments. In modern times there were additional problems deriving from the introduction of secular laws governing marriage. In some countries marriages were not allowed before a certain age. Often, the marriage had to be recorded by the state registrar before the religious ceremony could take place. Such laws were binding on all citizens.[62]

If Jews married earlier than the prescribed age or did not register with the state authorities, their marriage was not recognized by the state. Thus, if the husband in a halakhically valid marriage wanted to dissolve the union, he could go to the civil court and declare that the marriage had taken place in violation of the law of the state. The marriage would be annulled, and he would be free to leave his wife and remarry in civil court. The wife, however, would become an *agunah*, completely dependent for her freedom on the whim of the husband who had deserted her. Of course, the wife might follow the same procedure

62. Cf. Freimann, op. cit., pp. 218–219, 314, etc.

and have the marriage dissolved in civil court. That would enable her to marry another man according to the law of the country, but under Jewish law she and her new husband would be committing adultery, with all the halakhic implications for themselves and their offspring. What was to be done if these things were happening in violation of the *takkanot* of the communities?

The problem, in essence, was the same one we have encountered already in connection with the *takkanah* of Rabban Gamliel the Elder, who ordered that once a husband sent a *get* to his wife through a *shaliah* (messenger) he could not cancel the authorization without the knowledge of the *shaliah* or his wife. Otherwise the wife might think that she was divorced when, in fact, the *get* had been annulled by her husband's withdrawal of its halakhic validity.[63] Upon which the Talmud asks the question: what if, in spite of the *takkanah* of Rabban Gamliel, the husband does cancel his authorization without the messenger's knowledge? According to the law of the Torah, he has the right to do that. Thus the *get* he sent is invalid, but neither the *shaliah* nor the wife knows it. Thinking she is a divorced woman, the wife might remarry, with all the tragic consequences of such a marriage. One of the answers given to the question – the one accepted as Halakhah – was: people who marry assume that the marriage is taking place in accordance with the rabbinical rules (as is implied by the phrase "in accordance with the laws of Moses and Israel"). If a husband violates any of those rules, the rabbis have the authority to annul the validity of his *kiddushin*. Thus, the wife becomes free, even though the *get* she received is a meaningless piece of paper.

Clearly, communities have the required halakhic authority to establish communal *takkanot* in matters of marriage. Once the acknowledged rabbinical court of a community or even a country actually introduces such regulations, it has the authority to annul *kiddushin* retroactively if the *takkanot* are violated.

This was the challenge to rabbis and communities through the ages as they struggled with the problem of the *agunah*: to establish adequate *takkanot* whose violation would bring about the retroactive annulment of

63. Gittin 33a.

a marriage. The precedents in the Talmud would seem to have provided a rather easy solution to the problem, but many outstanding Talmudic scholars refused to act on the principle of the rabbinical authority to annual *kiddushin* retroactively. They reasoned that contemporary rabbis were less qualified than the rabbis of Talmudic times. "We are not like the court of Rav Ami and Rav Ashi," they would argue. So, too, ruled the Rema.[64] And yet, an impressive number of outstanding and commanding halakhic authorities ruled differently. The well-known Gaonim of the eighth, ninth, and tenth centuries, among them Rabbi Sherira Gaon, Rav Judah, and Rav Hai, taught unequivocally that the rabbis of every generation have the right to annul marriages that took place against their will. The sages of Worms and Speyer, in the days of the Ravan and Rambam, followed in their footsteps.[65] The Mabit, one of the great authorities of the fifteenth century, declared that post-Gaonic rabbinical teachers, who since the days of the Gaonim opposed the annulment of *kiddushin*, were obviously unaware of their views, for the rulings of the Gaonim were not contained in any written work. The rabbis of later generations would have followed these rulings and practices if they had known about them.[66]

It is worth noting that those who hesitated to allow appropriate conditions in the *ketubah* were mostly dealing with isolated cases. On the other hand, where problems occurred more frequently, rabbis were more inclined to use their authority to establish needed *takkanot* and to invalidate *kiddushin* that took place in disobedience to their *takkanot*. In order to eliminate all misunderstandings, it was required that the regulations should clearly state that any violation of the rules would bring about the annulment of the marriage.

Nearer to our times, the Hatam Sofer agreed to the invalidation of the *kiddushin* as long as the couple had not lived together as man and wife. He reasoned that a rabbinical court may act on the principle of *hefker bet din hefker*, i.e., property expropriated by the ruling of a rabbinical court becomes ownerless. Accordingly, if a bridegroom espouses a wife

64. *Shulhan Arukh*, Even ha-Ezer 28, end.
65. See Freimann, p. 100.
66. Responsa, pt. II, par. 105.

in violation of an established *takkanah*, he loses his ownership over the *kesef* (object of value) with which he espoused her. Since he has thus given nothing of his own to the intended bride, a legally valid *kiddushin* has not taken place.

If *nissu'in* by *huppah* did take place, however, and the couple had lived together as husband and wife, the marriage had a much stronger basis, for according to the halakhah a wife may be acquired not just by *kesef* but also by the act of cohabitation. The Hatam Sofer maintained that in Talmudic times the rabbis had the power, when the prescribed rules were violated, to invalidate even such a marriage, by declaring the cohabitation to be an act of harlotry (*zenut*). In post-Talmudic times the rabbis no longer had this authority.[67] Therefore, the annulment of the original *kiddushin* of *kesef* (i.e., espousal by means of an object of value) accomplishes nothing. The marriage would still be legal because of the other form of *kiddushin* effected by the couple's living together as husband and wife.

It has rightly been pointed out that the Hatam Sofer's argument does not apply to the conditions of life in our times. *Kiddushin* by cohabitation is a halakhically valid concept, but it is only effective if the following conditions are met: (1) the bridegroom declares before the act that his intention is to espouse the bride by it as his wife; (2) two witnesses testify that cohabitation for the purpose of *kiddushin* actually took place; (3) the witnesses are appointed by the bridegroom specifically to be aware of the couple's seclusion for the intended purpose. All this would violate the sense of decency and ethical sensitivity in our generation. Undoubtedly, in our time people who marry rely completely on *kiddushin* by *kesef* as the halakhically legal basis of their marriage. Therefore, if any of the established *takkanot* (communal or rabbinical marriage regulations) is violated, the *kiddushin* may be annulled retroactively.[68]

The qualified applicability of conditional marriages argued by the Hatam Sofer and other outstanding Ashkenazi Talmudic authorities was disregarded, especially by some of the greatest Sefaradi scholars. At the beginning of the nineteenth century, the rabbi of Trieste sought to

67. Freimann, p. 314.

68. E.g., see my *Tenai be-Nissu'in u-ve-Get,* 2nd ed. p. 67.

introduce *takkanot*, and to annul marriages when they were disobeyed. His decision was supported by reference to the Hida, an outstanding halakhic authority.[69]

The rabbi of Trieste and the Hida both made use of the halakhic principle known as *le-migdar milta*, i.e., "to fence in against an evil." This principle has its source in the Talmudic discussion of whether the sages have the authority *la'akov davar min ha-Torah*, "to uproot something from the Torah." In case of need, it is declared, they may disregard any teaching of the Torah. According to one opinion, they only have the right to do so passively, by inaction; another view holds that they have the authority to do so even by active disregard. In the end the discussion concludes: *le-migdar milta shani*, "to fence in a matter is different," i.e., when an evil violates Torah principles, there is no difference of opinion;[70] in other words, when an evil violates a principle of the Torah, all agree that a law of the Torah may be uprooted in order to eliminate the evil. The rabbi of Trieste quoted the Rosh, one of the greatest halakhic authorities since the close of the Talmud, in support of his ruling. Because of the importance of the Rosh's words for all generations, we shall quote them here:

> Everyone who weds a wife does it [in such a manner] that the marriage takes place in agreement with their rulings [i.e., of the rabbis]. And in each generation people marry with the understanding that they are adhering to the rulings of their contemporary rabbis, who instituted them *le-migdar milta* ["to fence in the matter," i.e., to eliminate some evil]. All marriages become legally effective only in accordance with their *takkanot*. Even if a person should wed by cohabitation, the act is rendered harlotry [and the marriage annulled]. How much more so when the espousal of the wife was done by *kesef* [i.e., by handing her some object of value], when the principle of *hefker bet din* applies [i.e., the rabbinical court negates the bridegroom's ownership of the *kesef* given], and no *kiddushin* had taken place at all.[71]

69. Freimann, pp. 316–319.
70. Yevamot 90b.
71. Rosh, Responsa, 35:1.

Most revealing was the attitude of the Rashba. In one of his responsa he deals with a case that happened in his city. After discussing the matter with "our teachers," the Rashba says, he decided that it was right to annul the marriage. He even adds: "My teacher, the Ramban, agreed with me." But he concludes: "Nevertheless it is still necessary to consider the matter."[72] Yet in another responsa, discussing the same subject, he writes that if it is a matter of "*le-migdar milta* [fencing in against an evil], if the communities, or even a single community, wish to correct a situation, by all means let them protect their *takkanot* by also introducing the *takkanot* of retroactive annulment of the *kiddushin*."[73]

Actually, the inclusion of appropriate conditions in a marriage contract seems to be halakhically a rather simple matter, as the following discussion shows. Torah law says that the surviving brother is to marry the widow of a husband who dies without leaving any offspring. If he refuses to do so, the *halitzah* ceremony is performed. Without it, the widow is not free to enter into a new marriage. Apparently this law caused serious problems through the ages, for in some cases the surviving brother was a *mumar* (apostate) and refused to participate in the *halitzah* ceremony, or could not be found, or lived so far away that the cost of the trip would have been excessive, or was mentally disturbed and incapable of functioning. Such cases caused much hardship for the widows affected, and sometimes led them to disregard the Torah law and marry someone else, even though doing so was a transgression. In order to eliminate these problems, Rabbi Israel of Bruenn (usually referred to as M'hari Brin) added a condition to the *ketubah* specifying that the marriage would be annulled retroactively if the husband died childless and his surviving brother refused to submit to the *halitzah* ceremony.[74]

The *tenai* introduced by Rabbi Israel of Bruenn is not to be confused with a *tenai* specifying that the law of levirate marriage to the surviving brother or the obligation of *halitzah* was to be disregarded altogether. The Talmud clearly states that such a condition would violate what is

72. Responsa, 1206.
73. Ibid. 551.
74. Even ha-Ezer 157:4.

written in the Torah and thus would have no validity.[75] In the M'hari Brin's *ketubah*, the husband does not reject the biblical institution of levirate marriage or anything connected with it. On the contrary, he fully accepts the law of the Torah, but in order to protect his wife against a great deal of suffering should a specific situation arise, he declares that the marriage does not take legal effect right from the beginning. This is a simple arrangement in complete conformity with the general rules governing conditional contracts. Understandably, it was suggested that the operative principle of the *tenai* of the M'hari Brin should be extended to include other kinds of conditions necessary to safeguard the desired character of marriages.[76]

As for the halakhic validity of a *tenai* added to a marriage contract, Rabbi Kook, of blessed memory, wrote that the condition stands and is effective. However, rabbis should not arrange *tena'im* as a general practice, for this would erode the form of the mitzvah of marriage, the foundation of the sanctity of the Jewish family.[77]

Such fears hardly seem warranted nowadays, when social conditions and widespread permissiveness are severely shaking the Jewish family. On the contrary. The exploitation of the power to give a *get* by unscrupulous husbands, which has become a daily occurrence, causes a great deal of disillusionment with the quality of justice implicit in the marriage laws.

Several other halakhic principles were also utilized to annul *kiddushin* retroactively, if the situation demanded it. A discussion in the Talmud indicates that the problem dealt with by the M'hari Brin also occupied the Talmudic sages. The question is raised: if the brother of the deceased husband is a *mumar* and refuses to submit to the *halitzah* ceremony, shouldn't the marriage be dissolved retroactively and automatically, because it is quite obvious that the wife would never have agreed to the marriage if she had known that she would have to undergo such a trial? The question is answered with an idea that is already familiar from our previous discussion: a woman is willing to accept any husband because,

75. Yerushalmi, Bava Mezia 7:7.
76. See Freimann, p. 386.
77. Ibid., p. 392; see also my *Tenai be-Nissu'in u-ve-Get,* 2nd ed., p. 77.

as Resh Lakish said, "it is better to live in two than to live alone."[78] We pointed out in the earlier discussion that Resh Lakish's view had some meaning in a time when women were uneducated, could not earn a living, and had no social status. Completely dependent on marriage, they would, if need be, accept any husband. Quite clearly, the very idea would be insulting to the Jewish women of modern times.

Be that as it may, we learn an important principle from this Talmudic passage: *adata de-hakhe lo kiddsha nafsha*, i.e., there occasionally may arise a situation where one may be sure that the wife would never have accepted the *kiddushin* if she had been aware of the lot that would befall her. In such cases, there would be no need for conditions explicitly incorporated into the marriage contract. And indeed, about fifty years ago, a rabbi suggested "that in case a woman becomes an *agunah* the *kiddushin* should become invalid. The wife should not need a *get* even if she had lived together with her husband as is customary. One may adjudge it with certainty that it was not 'for this' that she agreed to the marriage, even if no condition had been made in advance. For there cannot be any greater calamity for a woman than to remain an *agunah* forever."[79]

There were other Talmudic precedents to be considered in the effort to solve the *agunah* problem. We have already discussed the *uvda de-Narash*, "the case of [the forced marriage of] Narash."[80] A minor girl had been given into marriage by her mother and brothers, as was the rabbinical rule when the father died. However, since a marriage to a minor was binding only rabbinically and had no biblical basis, the husband planned to remarry the girl when she reached the age of majority. At that time she was taken to the *huppah*, but before he could give her the *kiddushin*, another took her away by force and performed the *kiddushin* as required by the Torah. As a result, the young woman was now the legally married wife of the second man. But the rabbis said: "He acted improperly; we too shall treat him improperly." They declared the second man's *kiddushin* invalid and returned the woman to the first man.

78. Bava Kama 111a.
79. Freimann, p. 393.
80. Yevamot 110a.

The same principle of invalidating a *kiddushin* is used in the Talmud in another context. A man took a woman, hung her from a tree, and said to her: "Here is your *kiddushin*. If you accept it, I will let you go."[81] Since the woman accepted the *kesef kiddushin* (the article of monetary value given her for the purpose of espousal), even though it was under duress, she was held to be legally married to the man. But again the rabbis declared: "He acted improperly; we too shall deal with him improperly." They declared the *kiddushin* invalid. The woman was free, without a *get*, to go and marry whomever she pleased.[82]

As we now see, the Talmud itself offers three different grounds for annulling a *kiddushin*: (1) the precedent of the *takkanah* of Rabban Gamliel the Elder, namely, that a *get* sent to one's wife by the hand of a *shaliah* may not be cancelled without the knowledge of the messenger and the wife; (2) where the husband has a condition or causes a situation that would have made the wife reject the marriage if she had known about it beforehand; (3) where the husband acts *shelo ke-hogen* (improperly).

The differences are obvious. In the case of the *takkanah* of Rabban Gamliel, the husband had the biblical right to cancel the *get* even without the knowledge of his messenger or his wife. Because of the possible evil consequences of such action for the wife, who might think that she was divorced when in fact she was not, Rabban Gamliel eliminated the husband's original right.

In the second case, no initial condition was stated explicitly, but it is understood that it was one of the terms of the wife's agreement. In the third example, too, one acts on the basis of an implied condition of the Jewish marriage law, as if to say: this is not the way to wed a wife; it violates our principles of justice, etc. In the second example, the wife's interest and purpose determine that the self-understood *tenai* was violated. In the third example, the marriage is annulled because the husband violated basic principles of Jewish ethics that he undertook to obey when he said to the bride, "I wed thee *ke-dat Mosheh ve-Yisrael*

81. Bava Batra 48b.

82. Freimann, p. 107, quotes the Radbaz, who refers to the principle of "improper action" by the husband in dealing with the possibility of retroactive annulment.

[according to the law of Moses and Israel]."

Of these three Talmudic precedents for retroactively invalidating a marriage, one might think it would be easiest to apply the *takkanah* of Rabban Gamliel the Elder. After all, Rabban Gamliel's rule was explicitly stated in advance, whereas in the other two cases there were no known rules whose violation would bring about the annulment of the *kiddushin*. However, to adjudge the three examples in this manner would be a mistake. The *takkanah* of Rabban Gamliel was a rabbinical innovation to deny the husband a right granted him by the Torah. In the other two cases, the rabbis acted in order to safeguard certain ethical principles included in the formula *ke-dat Mosheh ve-Yisrael*, so far as they are essential for the Torah-ordained Jewish marriage. Once it was established that any of these principles had been violated, the *kiddushin* automatically became invalid. Of course, not everyone is qualified to decide whether a violation has occurred. In the examples before us, it was done by halakhic authority.

We have no intention of giving a halakhic ruling on how the *agunah* problem in our day should be solved. This is not the place for it.[83] It is, however, sad to contemplate the fact that, in spite of the continually deteriorating situation, nothing significant has been undertaken to solve the problem.[84] In order to do so, a rabbinical court would have to deliberate seriously on two questions:

1. What are the situations that may develop in a marriage regarding which one might rule that no normal woman would agree to such a marriage had she known what might befall her as a result?
2. What are the moral and ethical principles of the Torah that are automatically included in "the laws of Moses and Israel" as the basis of a Jewish marriage?

Neither of these determinations would have to be explicitly included in the *ketubah*.

83. Those who are interested may consult my work, *Tenai be-Nissu'in u-ve-Get.*

84. There are now rabbis who are attempting to meet the challenge by the arrangement of prenuptial agreements which may be enforced in the civil courts. Is this not a confession that a serious halakhic problem cannot be solved within the system of the Halakhah?!

One of the rabbis who agree to the retroactive annulment of *kiddushin* writes that one does it so that the people will know that the sages of the time are concerned about the well-being of the daughters of Israel and to build a fence against lawlessness.[85] Even though the words the rabbi was using are a quotation from the Talmud,[86] still…

How far removed we are from care and concern for the well-being of the daughters of Israel! The rabbinical establishment does not seem to pay much attention to the suffering, and often the disillusionment with Judaism itself, caused by its fear to accept halakhic responsibility for the solution of the present-day *agunah* problem. Its members seem indifferent to the many violations of the teachings of the Torah, especially in the areas of ethics and morality, that are due to the unresolved status of the *agunah* problem! Ultimately, the situation involves a high measure of *hillul Hashem* for which the rabbinical establishment is responsible. This, surely, is not halakhic Judaism.

85. Freimann, p. 332.
86. Ketubot 2a.

V Conclusions

We have found that there have been two phases in the status of women in Jewish tradition. The nonpersonal one, essentially determined by the social and economic conditions of an early society, was not much different from what could be observed in the non-Jewish cultures of the time. It was a condition tolerated by the Torah, but not instituted by Torah teaching and Torah values.

The second phase, which we called the personal status of the woman, acknowledged the value and dignity of the female personality. It was taught and demanded by Torah ideals. It even led to halakhic innovations out of concern for the rights and welfare of women. Unfortunately, the second phase did not follow upon the first in historical development. Moreover, the personal status did not arise as a historical reality, especially in the area of religious ritual, after the overcoming of the mores deriving from the conditions that had determined women's nonpersonal status. The two value systems existed side by side for many centuries, and to some extent even into our own time, without adequate realization that Torah teachings were not being given adequate realization in the daily life of the people.

Most revealing in this respect is the opinion of Rav. He taught: "Do not marry two women [polygamy was still practiced]." Explains Rashi: "Because they join to plot against you." Rav continues: "However, if you did marry two, also marry a third one." Once again Rashi explains: "The third one will reveal the plotting of the other two."[1]

Yet the same Rav also ruled that even though, according to biblical

1. Pesahim 113a.

law, a man has the right to appoint a *shaliah* (representative) to espouse a wife on his behalf, he should not do so, because the Torah says, "And thou shalt love thy neighbor as thyself." What Rav means is that if a man did not see the woman before she became his wife, he might turn out not to like her after the marriage, and then he would be in violation of the commandment to love his neighbor.

In these two sayings of Rav the two systems confirm each other. The Torah teaches: "thou shalt love thy neighbor as thyself." But on the other hand, there were also the actual conditions of the lives of the people. The teaching demanding the acknowledgment of the woman's personal status had not as yet overcome all the consequences of the early impersonal status.

Let us recall some of the examples. According to the Halakhah as stated in the Talmud, women are no less obligated than men to say grace after a meal. Accordingly, woman should have the right to say *Birkat ha-Mazon* even for men, who would fulfill their own obligation by listening to their reading it for them. Nothing in the Talmud contravenes such a ruling. Yet post-Talmudic codifiers of the Halakhah ruled that women could not act in this manner on behalf of men. As we saw, the reason for such exclusion appears in two forms. One held that women have no part in the obligations that follow from the principle that "all Jews are responsible for each other." The second, based on the personal status of women (and thus even more objectionable), held that women do not have an adequately respected position to be authorized to perform the religious obligation of saying grace on behalf of men. Even more characteristic is the opinion of Rabbenu Nissim (Ran), who distinguishes between the inclusion of a woman in the required quorum for *zimun* (the saying of grace jointly, for which three persons are required) and the reading of the Megillah. Women are excluded from *zimun*, according to him, but he had to acknowledge not only that women have the authority to read the Megillah even for men, but that they may be included in the required quorum for public reading. And now comes the surprising distinction: the blessing before the reading requires no change in its formula, no matter how many people participate in it. Therefore, the text of the blessing will not attract attention to the female presence, whereas *zimun* in the required quorum of three is added to the regular text of the grace, and thus the presence of a woman would be noted.

In other words, women are excluded from *zimun* because one must not call attention to their presence. We also noted that notwithstanding the clear fact that on mishnaic authority it is stated that women are obligated to read the Megillah and are qualified to do so, a complicated discussion as to whether women are obligated to read the Megillah is conducted by later post-Talmudic authorities, arguing against the Mishnah's position on the basis of a Tosefta whose opinion would not normally be accepted.

Finally, we find a compromise solution, not fully recognized in the *Shulhan Arukh*, that while women are not to read the Megillah themselves, they should listen to its reading. Another compromise solution is that women may read the Megillah to women. Equally remarkable and revealing is Rashi's opinion that women may not participate in *zimun*, not even with their husbands, because "the association with them is improper." Even more surprising is the ruling in the *Shulhan Arukh* about women putting on *tefillin* for prayer. The commandment of *tefillin*, as we have seen, is the foundation for the rule that women are not obligated to fulfill *mizvot aseh she-ha-zeman geramah*, positive commandments connected with the time of the day, the week, or the season. Yet it was also ruled that if women wish, they may obligate themselves concerning even those commandments. Now come some post-Talmudic authorities, basing themselves on a private post-Talmudic view that women should not be allowed to put on *tefillin*. And thus the ruling appears in the *Shulham Arukh* that women should not be permitted to put on *tefillin* because they are not sufficiently careful about their bodily hygiene.

One cannot help asking how such attitudes and rulings can be reconciled with Torah principles that a man should love his wife as himself and honor her more than himself, or the teaching that a house is blessed mainly because of the wife, and many others in the same spirit. There is only one explanation: in spite of the Torah ideals and teachings, the views about the female personality, and the social conditions that determined them, persisted from the phase of the nonpersonal status of women. If Rashi says that it was not proper to sit together with women to say grace, or the *Shulhan Arukh* rules, with reference to the menstrual period, that women do not take sufficient care to keep their bodies clean, these were indeed the conditions at those times. Because the mores of the nonpersonal phase persisted, it was indeed difficult to accept the idea that women could read the Megillah for men or were important enough to say grace, for this would have meant that men could fulfill their duties in cooperation with such incomplete personalities.

At the same time, we ought to understand that these and all similar rulings are not based on the plain and clear meaning of the classical halakhic text. In fact, they are often deviations from it, creating exceptions to normally valid principles. Often, we are confronted with original halakhic principles, but with rulings imposed upon Halakhah by the prevailing time-dependent culture that made it necessary to respect the existing male-female relationship.

The power of the influence of the nonpersonal status of women was indicated by the saying of Rabbi Eliezer, according to which a person who teaches his daughter Torah is as if he had taught her promiscuity. This in itself is sufficient to show the survival of the values of the nonpersonal status. But how much more powerful does such survival prove itself when one learns Rabbi Eliezer's opinion about women from the text in the Jerusalem Talmud, which states, as we noted, "Let the Torah be burnt but not be handed to women." Notwithstanding all this, Rabbi Eliezer's ruling was generally followed, in most religious circles, up to our own days.

The most deplorable aspect of the present-day situation in matters of Halakhah and religious ritual is the fact that even though the personal status of women has been fully achieved in the social sphere, little attention has been given to the halakhic consequences. Many of the rulings discussed above, which in effect impose the surviving mores of the nonpersonal stage upon the Halakhah, have remained untouched. Unfortunately, ignoring current developments in this way reflects a nonhalakhic attitude. Instead of examining the basis of certain *takkanot* (rules and regulations) to see whether they still have meaning and purpose, the rabbinical establishment is afraid of any change and anything new. In certain areas, of course, life itself has taken over.

We noted that Maimonides, on the basis of a source in the Talmud, ruled that a husband should not allow his wife to leave their home more than once or twice a month. I strongly doubt that this law is still observed in religious circles. Are there still any families whose daughters behave in accordance with the biblical teaching that "the honor of a king's daughter is inside a corner of her house"? But let us also realize that the contemporary practice is not a violation of the teaching of Maimonides. The Rambam was right. In the time of the Talmud and, obviously, in his own day too, such was proper behavior for Jewish women. It would be completely meaningless today.

At the same time, we cannot help noting the text-addicted inconsistent attitude of the religious establishment. Daughters of religious families and young wives study and learn all kinds of professions. They work in offices, business enterprises, and organizations together with men. Many of them earn the living for the family while their husbands study Torah in a *kollel*. Yet, at the same time, serious objections are raised against women being elected to public office. At the time of this writing the rabbinate in Israel strongly opposes the election of women to religious councils, because one of the responsibilities of such councils is the election of rabbis in their cities. As we have shown, there is no halakhic basis whatever for opposing women's participation in public offices, councils, and representative bodies.

How far we have come from the ethics of authentic Halakhah is well illustrated by two examples. We have found that in recognition of the personal human dignity of women, major changes and innovations were introduced even into some biblical laws. For instance, Talmudic and post-Talmudic rulings and regulations ensured that women would be treated justly in matters of inheritance. This meant that the early laws were effectively abolished. As we have shown, those laws were valid in their own time but became severely discriminatory and intolerable once woman's personal status had been acknowledged. And yet to this day, when a husband bequeaths his possessions to his wife in his last will and testament, the Israeli rabbinate will call the children and ask them whether they are willing to renounce their father's inheritance to their mother. What could be more farcical than such a procedure!

One recalls that Rabbi Judah ha-Nasi called in his sons before his death and urged them to be extremely careful in all matters concerning respect for their mother. And before him, when Rabbi Joseph heard the footsteps of his mother coming, he would rise out of respect for the approaching divine presence.

But by far more objectionable is the utter disregard for the numerous halakhic innovations introduced by Talmudic teachers to protect the wife against the possible harmful consequences of the husband's behavior in matters of divorce. These innovations would enable us to introduce appropriate *tenaim* (conditions) into the marriage contract (*ketubah*) that would solve the many problems arising from a broken-down marriage. But nothing is being done, and the result is the untold suffering of the many wives who are exposed to the willfulness of their husbands. The situation is especially serious in Israel, where marriages and divorces are under the authority of the rabbinate. The prevailing conditions are not due to Halakhah; on the contrary, they are in violation of fundamental principles of halakhic ethics.

Unfortunately, the problem that we are discussing is not limited to the subject of the status of women in Judaism. It is a problem that involves the entire area of present-day religious faith. The so-called drift to the right is a drift towards a naïve, unquestioning spirituality. In essence, it is a drift away from authentic Halakhah. Because of this it would be useless to place our hopes on the rabbinical establishment either in Israel or in the Diaspora. Just because of this we need rabbis who are *talmidei hakhamim* (Talmudic scholars) with an adequate worldly education, who are seriously concerned and troubled by the inadequate regard for the problems of contemporary Jewish religious life; whose sense of rabbinical responsibility will give them courage to speak out; and who, at least in the area of their influence, will introduce the halakhic changes that are required in recognition of the human dignity of the Jewish woman of today. Perhaps this will lead to a gradual halakhic renewal that will ultimately re-establish Judaism as *Torat Hayyim* – a Torah of Life.

Glossary

Words set in SMALL CAPS are defined elsewhere in the Glossary.

Bah. Rabbi Joel Sirkes (1561–1640). Poland. Author of responsa and of *Bayit Hadash* commentary on the TUR.

Behag. The anonymous author of the *Halakhot Gedolot*, a summary of Talmudic law often attributed to Simeon Kayyara of Basra (ninth century CE).

Even ha-Ezer. The third major section of the TUR and the SHULHAN ARUKH, treating all aspects of marriage and divorce law.

Hagah. A comment or gloss to a main body of text. Especially referring to the glosses of REMA on the SHULHAN ARUKH.

Halakhah. Jewish law. Derived from the Hebrew word meaning "walk, go." Halakhah is both the set of normative religious standards and the traditional process for determining those standards.

Kesef Mishneh. One of the principal commentaries to the RAMBAM's *Mishneh Torah.* Written by Joseph Karo (1488–1575), the author of the SHULHAN ARUKH. The major aim of the *Kesef Mishneh* is to identify the Talmudic sources underlying the halakhic rulings of the *Mishneh Torah.*

Maggid Mishneh. One of the principal commentaries to the RAMBAM's *Mishneh Torah.* Written by Vidal Yom Tov of Tolosa in the fourteenth century. He attempts to resolve difficult passages and often defends the *Mishneh Torah* against the criticism of Rabbi Abraham ben David of Posquieres (Rabad).

Midrash. A rabbinic method of analysis or commentary typically employed in relation to the Bible. The linguistic root of the term means "search, investigate." Midrash is a process of deriving or uncovering layers of meaning, legal implications, "historical" details, etc., over and beyond the strictly literal sense of the text. Midrashic works usually take the form of either a sustained homiletical presentation on a certain theme or a line-by-line exegesis of a biblical text.

Midrash Rabbah. The general name given to a set of midrashic works on the Pentateuch and five books of the Writings (Song of Songs, Ruth, Lamentations, Ecclesiastes, Esther). These collections achieved their final literary form between the fifth and twelfth centuries C.E. Each book (e.g., Genesis Rabbah, Ruth Rabbah) is an independent composition, and the style and purposes of each can vary considerably.

Rabbenu Tam. Rabbi Jacob ben Meir (1096–1171). France. A grandson of RASHI. R. Tam was the most authoritative rabbinical figure of his time throughout France, Germany, and other parts of the Jewish world. Besides his status as a decisor of HALAKHAH, he was the principal force behind the creation of the system of Talmudic analysis known as TOSAFOT.

Rambam. Rabbi Moses ben Maimon, known also as Maimonides (1135–1204). Spain and Egypt. Rambam is probably the most well-known Jew of the Middle Ages. His influence on the history of Judaism as halakhist and philosopher has been profound. His main works include the *Commentary to the Mishnah*, the *Guide to the Perplexed*, his major philosophical statement, and most importantly the Mishneh Torah, probably the most comprehensive account of Jewish law ever produced.

Rashba. Rabbi Solomon ben Abraham (1235–1310). Spain. He is best known for his tremendous production of responsa, numbering well over 10,000. In these he addressed questions, sent to him from all over the Jewish world, on all types of legal issues. He also dealt with problems of exegesis and philosophy. In addition, Rashba commented extensively on the Talmud.

Rashbam. Rabbi Samuel ben Meir (1080–1174). France. A grandson of RASHI and the older brother of RABBENU TAM. Prominent both as a Talmudist and as a biblical commentator in the tradition of his grandfather. With Bible his approach was to stress the literal, straightforward meaning of the text.

Rashi. Rabbi Solomon ben Isaac (1040–1105). France. The premier commentator on Bible and Talmud. His work is renowned for its brevity and clarity. Rashi's commentary on the Talmud helped make it accessible to the masses of Jews and became virtually synonymous with Talmud study.

Rema. Rabbi Moses ben Israel Isseries (1525–1572). Poland. One of the leading halakhic authorities for Ashkenazic Jewry (Germany, Eastern Europe, Russia). He added supplementary notes to the SHULHAN ARUKH, a code of law which most often reflected Sefardic practice (Spain, Western Europe, North Africa). By bringing in Ashkenazic traditions and customs he made it possible for the SHULHAN ARUKH to become a universally accepted authority.

Rif. Rabbi Issac ben Jacob Alfasi (1013–1103). North Africa. Author of the *Sefer Halakhot*, the most important code of Jewish law prior to the RAMBAM's *Mishneh Torah*. The Rif's work was an attempt to summarize and give the final rulings of Talmudic discussions. In doing so he tried to preserve the language and structure of the Talmud as much as possible.

Rivash. Rabbi Isaac ben Sheshet (1326–1408). Spain and North Africa. Author of a large numbers of responsa. His writings were consulted extensively by Joseph Karo in the formation of the SHULHAN ARUKH.

Rosh. Rabbi Asher ben Yehiel (1250–1327). France, Germany, and Spain. Outstanding halakhic authority and Talmudic scholar. His legal decisions were one of the three principal sources upon which the rulings of the SHULHAN ARUKH were based. His schools also produced extensive TOSAFOT. One of the few rabbis to exercise direct influence in his own lifetime over Ashkenazic and Sefardic Jewry.

Shoftim. The Hebrew name for the biblical book of Judges.

Shulhan Arukh. Hebrew for "Prepared Table." Composed by Joseph Karo with additions by REMA and first published in 1565. This work became the major authority for halakhic practice throughout the Jewish world. It is divided into the same four major divisions as the TUR of Jacob ben Asher. It contains concise rulings in all areas of Jewish tradition still directly relevant after the destruction of the Second Temple.

Sifre. Early collections of MIDRASH on the biblical books of Numbers and Deuteronomy. Probably edited toward the end of the fourth century C.E. in the Land of Israel. Contains both legal and homiletical material.

Targum Yonatan. An Aramaic translation of the second section of the Hebrew Bible, which is termed Prophets. This translation originated in the land of Israel and was probably redacted by the seventh century C.E. Its purpose was to make these biblical books accessible to Jews who were no longer fluent in Hebrew. More than a literal translation, it contains a great deal of midrashic and legendary material.

Tashbaz. The three-part collected responsa of Rabbi Simeon ben Zemah Duran (1361–1444). North Africa. His writings touch on a very wide range of topics. Besides rulings on HALAKHAH, the author wrote on issues pertaining to history, philosophy, mathematics, astronomy, and the like.

Tosafot. A method of Talmudic analysis which developed in the rabbinical academies of France and Germany from the twelfth to the fourteenth century. These schools produced an extensive literature of Talmudic commentary, and this method of study spread throughout most parts of the Jewish world. The standard editions of the Talmud have RASHI's commentary on one side of the page and a set of Tosafot on the other side.

Tur. Also known as the *Arba'ah Turim*, "The Four Rows." Major halakhic compendium written by Jacob ben Asher (1270–1340) in Spain. The TUR became particularly significant for its organizational structure, which was adopted by almost every subsequent code of Jewish law, most importantly the SHULHAN ARUKH. It is divided into four main sections: Orah Hayyim (everyday ritual, prayer, Sabbath and holidays); YOREH DE'AH (dietary rules, sexual regulations, laws of conversion, mourning, and various other topics); EVEN HA-EZER (laws of marriage and divorce); and Hoshen Mishpat (civil and judicial procedure).

Yoreh De'ah. The second major section of the TUR and the SHULHAN ARUKH. It includes a wide variety of subjects, such as dietary rules, restrictions relating to idolatry, sexual regulations, laws of vows and oaths, honoring parents, charity, conversion, and mourning practices.